GLISH

SKILLS

se for Intermediate Students

By the same author

Sixty Steps to Précis
Poetry and Prose Appreciation
Essay and Letter-writing
A First Book in Comprehension, Précis and Composition
The Carters of Greenwood *(Cineloops)*
Detectives from Scotland Yard *(Longman Structural Readers, Stage 1)*
Car Thieves *(Longman Structural Readers, Stage 1)*
Worth A Fortune *(Longman Structural Readers, Stage 2)*
April Fools' Day *(Longman Structural Readers, Stage 2)*
Operation Mastermind *(Longman Structural Readers, Stage 3)*
Professor Boffin's Umbrella *(Longman Structural Readers, Stage 2)*
Question and Answer: Graded Aural/Oral Exercises
For and Against
Reading and Writing English. A First Year Programme for Children
Look, Listen and Learn! Sets 1–4 An Integrated Course for Children

NEW CONCEPT ENGLISH
Uniform with this Volume:
First Things First: An Integrated Course for Beginners
Practice and Progress: An Integrated Course for Pre-Intermediate Students
Fluency in English: An Integrated Course for Advanced Students

NEW CONCEPT ENGLISH *in two Volume edition*
First Things First Parts 1–2
Practice and Progress Parts 1–2

NEW CONCEPT ENGLISH

DEVELOPING SKILLS
An Integrated Course For Intermediate Students

L. G. ALEXANDER
Illustrations by Michael ffolkes, Graham and Gus

LONGMAN

Longman Group Limited
London

Associated companies, branches and representatives
throughout the world.

First published 1964
New impression 1974 (twice)

ISBN 0 582 52331 1

ACKNOWLEDGMENTS

We are indebted to the Cambridge Local Examinations' Syndicate
for permission to quote material from past examination papers.

Printed and Bound in Great Britain by McCorquodale (Newton) Ltd, Newton–le-Willows, Merseyside

CONTENTS

To the Teacher

Language Learning and the Intermediate Student

When a student has completed a pre-intermediate course, he enters a period of consolidation and expansion. What has been learnt so far must be practised constantly. At the same time, the student must learn to come to terms with wider English. He will still have intensive practice in the four skills, *understanding*, *speaking*, *reading* and *writing*, but many of the exercises he will be doing will be less mechanical.

At this level, there is less need for pattern control and contextualization. Now that the foundations have been laid, the student is in a position to cope with new sentence patterns as and when they occur. However, it is still necessary for the student to work from specially-written multi-purpose texts if he is to be trained systematically in speech and writing.

Students working at this level often wish to sit for academic examinations like the Cambridge Lower Certificate. Now it is a curious paradox that formal examinations often hinder rather than help a student to learn a language. However, there should be no need to work at cross-purposes: it is quite possible for the student to go on learning a language and to prepare for an examination at the same time. It must be clearly understood that a formal examination with its bias towards the written language will only exert a pernicious influence on language learning when it is regarded as an end in itself. When the teacher makes it his aim to get his class through an examination and no more, he will undoubtedly fail to teach the language properly. An examination must always be regarded as something secondary, a by-product which the student will take in his stride. It must never be regarded as an end in itself. An intermediate course should not only enable a student to go on learning English systematically, but should, incidentally, enable him to pass an examination without special preparation.

About this Course

Basic Aims

1. To provide a comprehensive course for adult or secondary students who have completed a pre-intermediate course. The course contains sufficient material for one academic year's work. It is assumed that the student will receive about four hours' instruction each week: i.e. four one-hour lessons on four separate occasions, or two 'double periods' each consisting of two hours or ninety minutes. The student will receive most of his training in the classroom and will be required to do a certain amount of extra work in his own time.
2. To continue the student's training in the four skills: *understanding*, *speaking*, *reading* and *writing*—in that order. In this respect, the course sets out to do two things: to provide material which will be suitable for aural/oral practice and which can also be used to train the student systematically to write English.
3. To provide the student with a book which will enable him to *use* the language.
4. To provide the teacher with material which will enable him to conduct each lesson with a minimum of preparation.
5. To enable the teacher and the student to work entirely from a single volume without the need for additional 'practice books'.
6. To enable students to sit for the Cambridge Lower Certificate examination at the end of the course if they wish to do so. This aim must be regarded as coincidental to the main purpose of training students in the four language skills.

For Whom the Course is Intended

This course should be found suitable for:
1. Adult or secondary students who have completed *Practice and Progress: An Integrated Course for Pre-Intermediate Students*, or who have completed *any* other pre-intermediate course.
2. Schools and Language Institutes where 'wastage' caused by irregular attendance and late starters is a problem.
3. Intermediate students who wish to study on their own.

How Much Knowledge has been Assumed?

The material in *Practice and Progress*, the pre-intermediate course which precedes this one, has been designed to 'overlap' this course. Students who have completed it will have no difficulty whatever in continuing where they left off.

Students who have learnt English from other courses and who now wish to continue their studies with this course should have a fair working knowledge of the items listed below.

Assumed Knowledge

Aural/Oral
1. The ability to understand short passages of English (narrative and descriptive) spoken at normal speed.
2. The ability to answer questions which require short or extended answers.

3. The ability to ask questions to elicit short or extended answers.
4. The ability to use orally a fair number of elementary sentence patterns.
5. The ability to reproduce orally the substance of a short passage of English after having heard it several times and read it.

Reading
1. The ability to read a short passage of English (up to 200 words in length) aloud. The student should have a fair grasp of the *rhythm* of the language (stress and intonation) even if he is unable to pronounce unfamiliar words correctly.
2. The ability to read silently and understand works of fiction of the level of Longmans' Structural Readers Series, Stage 6. The student's passive vocabulary range should be in the region of 2000 words (*structural* and *lexical*).

Writing
1. *Word Order*
The ability to write *simple*, *compound* and *complex* sentences.
2. *Comprehension*
The ability to answer in writing simple questions on a passage of English.
3. *Précis*
The ability to connect ideas from notes that have been provided so as to form a complete paragraph.
4. *Composition*
The ability to write a short composition of about 150 words based on ideas that have been provided.
5. *Letter-writing*
Knowledge of the lay-out of the personal letter. The ability to write a short letter based on ideas that have been provided.

Command of Language
1. *Grammar* (*Key Structures*)
The course presupposes that the student has covered the elementary and pre-intermediate groundwork. It is clearly recognized, however, that further instruction and practice are required.
2. *Usage* (*Special Difficulties*)
The student should be familiar with a number of words that are often confused or misused and a limited number of idiomatic expressions.

A Description of the Course

The course consists of the following:

One text book (to be used by teachers and students).
Set 1. Four 5 in. (13 cm.) long-playing tapes (length: 900 feet), recorded at $3\frac{3}{4}$ i.p.s. (9·5 cm. p.s.), on which drills have been recorded.
Set 2. Five $4\frac{1}{4}$ in. (11 cm.) long-playing tapes (length: 600 feet), recorded at $3\frac{3}{4}$ i.p.s. (9·5 cm. p.s.), on which multi-purpose texts have been recorded.
Recorded drills: Tapescript.
Supplementary written exercises: Multiple choice.

General Arrangement of Material
This course is divided into three Units the first two of which are preceded by searching tests. Each Unit consists of twenty passages which become longer and

more complex as the course progresses. Detailed instructions to the student, together with worked examples, precede each Unit.

The passages are multi-purpose texts. Each passage will be used to train the student in the following: aural comprehension; oral practice; reading aloud; oral composition; extended oral exercises; dictation; comprehension; précis; composition; grammar.

Instructions and Worked Examples

These precede each Unit and should be read very carefully. The successful completion of this course depends entirely on the student's ability to carry out the instructions given.

Pre-unit Tests

A searching test, based on material already studied, precedes Units 1 and 2. This will make it possible for students to find their own level and enable them to begin at any point in the book. At the same time, the student who works through the course systematically from beginning to end is not expected to make too sudden a jump between Units. The tests should enable the teacher to assess how much the students have learnt. If they are found to be too long, they should be divided into manageable compartments.

The Passages

An attempt has been made to provide the student with passages which are as interesting and as varied in subject-matter as possible. Each passage will be used as the basis for aural/oral and written work. The approximate length of the passages in each Unit is as follows:

Unit 1 : 250 words.
Unit 2 : 350 words.
Unit 3 : 530 words.

Oral Exercises

Oral exercises are not included in the book itself and must be supplied by the teacher. They may be along the lines suggested in the section on How to Use This Course.

Comprehension Questions

The student will elicit specific information from each passage.

Précis

Work has been graded as follows:
Unit 1 : The students will be trained to write notes by means of comprehension questions on the passages. The students will answer the comprehension questions in note form and then connect their notes to form a paragraph. Connecting words have not been provided.
Units 2 & 3 : The students will now be in a position to elicit specific information from each passage and write a précis on their own.

Composition

Work has been graded as follows:
Unit 1 : Alternating exercises.
a Expanding sentences to form a paragraph of about 150 words.

b Writing compositions in three paragraphs on set plans in which the ideas have been provided. About 200 words.

Unit 2: Alternating exercises.

a Expanding ideas to construct a plan. Writing a composition of about 250 words which is based on each plan.

b Writing compositions in three or four paragraphs based on set plans in which ideas have been provided. About 250 words.

Unit 3: Writing compositions of about 300 words on topics suggested by the passages. The student will be required to construct his own plan and to provide his own ideas.

Letter-writing
Work has been graded as follows:

Unit 1: Writing letters based on ideas which have been provided.

Units 2 & 3: Writing letters on set topics.

Vocabulary Exercises
Exercises in explaining words and phrases as they are used in the passages are given in all three Units.

Key Structures and Special Difficulties
All the exercises on Key Structures (Essential Grammar) and Special Difficulties (Usage) are derived from each passage. There are grammar exercises in Units 1 and 2 only. The exercises given are based largely on patterns which were fully explained in the pre-intermediate course *Practice and Progress.*

Cross-references
Cross-references have been included to enable the student to refer to material he has already learnt and to draw useful comparisons. Students who previously studied *Practice and Progress* are advised to refer to it when in difficulty. In the text, cross-references are in heavy type and are indicated in the following manner:

a 1 KS (=KEY STRUCTURE) These letters are followed by a page number and sometimes a paragraph reference: e.g. 1 KS 47b. The figure '1' indicates that the reference is to a section in the previous volume *Practice and Progress.*

b KS (=KEY STRUCTURE) The omission of the figure '1' indicates that the reference is to a section of the present volume.

c 1 SD (=SPECIAL DIFFICULTY) These letters are followed by a page number and sometimes a paragraph reference: e.g. 1 SD 52c. The figure '1' indicates that the reference is to a section in the previous volume *Practice and Progress.*

d SD (=SPECIAL DIFFICULTY) The omission of the figure '1' indicates that the reference is to a section of the present volume.

Multiple Choice Questions
Multiple Choice Questions have been added to Units 2 and 3 to provide additional help for students who are specifically preparing for the Cambridge Lower Certificate examination. In this form of comprehension exercise, the student is asked to select the correct answer from a number of suggested answers. A separate publication consisting entirely of multiple choice exercises based on each text is also available.

How to Use this Course

Allocation of Time

Ideally, two classroom lessons of approximately 50 minutes each should be spent on each text. The first lesson should be devoted to Guided Conversation; the second to Composition and Language Study. This means that there is enough material in this book for 120 lessons. However, you may choose to spend only *one* classroom lesson on each text—in which case, every lesson may be devoted to Guided Conversation and a selection of written exercises may be set as homework. Your first task is to decide how much time you have in your programme in relation to the material available in the course.

The suggestions given below outline the basic steps in each lesson. You may decide to follow them closely, adapt them to suit your style of teaching, or reject them altogether—BUT PLEASE READ THEM FIRST!

Lesson 1: Guided Conversation

Books required:

> *Developing Skills* (for teachers and students)
> *Recorded Drills Tapescript* (for teachers only)

The Stages of the Lesson

1 Aural/Oral Presentation:	about 15 minutes
2 Question and Answer Practice:	about 10 minutes
3 Pattern Drill:	about 5 minutes
4 Oral Reconstruction:	about 10 minutes
5 Talking Points, Singing, Games, Story-telling, etc:	about 10 minutes

Let's see what each step involves:
1 *Aural/Oral Presentation*:
  a Listening (Books shut)
  b Intensive Reading (Books open)
  c Listening (Books shut)
  d Reading Aloud (Books open)

a Listening (Books shut). Play the recording or read the passage once. The students should *listen* and try to understand as much as they can.
b Intensive Reading (Books open). Read the test in small units (e.g. a sentence at a time, or less) making sure the students *really* understand it. Rather than give direct explanations, try to get as much information as possible from the students. (Think of it as 'a corkscrew operation'!) Explanations should be given entirely in English, but don't carry direct-method teaching to absurd lengths. If your students fail to understand in spite of all your efforts, translate briefly and move

on. Remember, if you don't translate a particular difficulty, then someone in the class will!

c Listening (Books shut). Play the recording or read the passage once more.

d Reading Aloud (Books open). Ask a few individual students to read small portions of the text.

2 *Question and Answer Practice*

Question and answer practice should be based mainly on the text. However, you may frequently vary this with questions which relate to the student's own experience. If you find it difficult to ask questions spontaneously, prepare yourself in advance. Questions should be asked individually round the class—preferably at speed. Two exercises are suggested:

    a Mixed Questions

    b Asking Questions in Pairs

a Mixed Questions. General comprehension questions may be asked. Here, for instance, are a number of questions which relate to Text 1.

Teacher: What are pumas like?

            They're like cats, aren't they?

            Where are they found? etc.

b Asking Questions in Pairs. Train the student to ask a question using an auxiliary verb and then to ask *precisely the same question again* preceding it with a question word.

Teacher: Ask me if pumas are like cats.

Student: Are pumas like cats?

Teacher: What . . . (Always provide the Question word.)

Student: What are pumas like? etc.

3 *Pattern Drill*

Drill the main language point which has been introduced in the text. Use the publication entitled 'Developing Skills, Recorded Drills: Tapescript' for this purpose. Here, for instance, is part of the drill which relates to Text 2:

Teacher: I've borrowed George's car.

Student: You're always borrowing George's car.

Teacher: He's got into trouble.

Student: He's always getting into trouble. etc.

The students may be trained to answer in chorus or groups, or the drill may be conducted a number of times rapidly round the class with individual students responding. A brief grammatical explanation may be given before the drill is conducted. If a language-laboratory is available, this will be adequate preparation for further practice. However, it must be stressed that a laboratory is by no means indispensable: it is quite possible to do all the drilling live in the classroom. Alternatively, teachers who have tape-recorders may choose to play the drills in class.

4 *Oral Reconstruction*

Write a number of brief notes ('key words') on the blackboard summarising the subject-matter of the last paragraph (*not* the whole story!). Now invite individual pupils to reconstruct the text by referring to the notes. The students should be encouraged to speak without interruption for short periods and should try to use as many as possible of the expressions, structures, etc., of the original story.

Here, for instance, are some notes which relate to Text 1:

1 Hunt—village.	5 Trail—dead deer—rabbits.
2 Woman—blackberries—large cat.	6 Paw prints—fur.
3 Ran away—experts confirmed—not attack.	7 Cat-like noises—business man.
4 Search difficult—morning/evening.	8 *Was* a puma—where from?
	9 Not zoo—private collector.

5 Talking Points, Singing, Games, Story-telling, etc.
The final part of the Guided Conversation Lesson should be devoted to free conversation. Where the text immediately suggests a subject or subjects for general discussion, individual students should be invited to speak impromptu. Here, for instance, are a few talking points suggested by Text 1.
a Which animals you like/dislike most and why.
b Describe a visit to a zoo.
c Your attitude to zoos: is it right to put animals into cages?
Obviously, not all texts provide suitable material for conversation. Where a general discussion is not possible, the lesson may end with any one of the following activities:
a Singing: Teach the class traditional or modern British and American songs. Any good song book may be used for this purpose.
b Games: Well-known parlour games like 'Twenty Questions' are always popular with students. A book like 'Language-teaching Games and Contests' by W. R. Lee (O.U.P.) is full of excellent ideas.
c Story-telling: You may occasionally read a story to the class—providing it is roughly within the students' structural/lexical range. Many of the titles in the Longman Simplified English Series are suitable for this purpose.

Lesson 2: Composition and Language Study

As has already been indicated, this entire lesson may be omitted and a selection of written exercises may, instead, be set as homework. If this approach is adopted, then *either* the Précis *or* the Composition *must always be set*. Needless to say, more satisfactory results will be obtained where a complete classroom lesson can be devoted to written exercises.

Books Required:

> *Developing Skills* (for teachers and students)
> *Supplementary Written Exercises* (for teachers)

The exercises may be tackled in the order in which they are given. While the students are writing, you may go round the class helping individuals. Exercises not completed in class time, may be set as homework. The written exercises become more demanding and time-consuming as the student progresses through the course. However, it is not necessary to complete every single exercise. Note that additional multiple choice practice is provided in a separate publication.

Dictations
Depending on the amount of time available, dictations should be given frequently. A few sentences taken from a passage the students have already studied may be

dictated. The students may correct their own work by comparing their version with the passage.

Pre-Unit Tests
These should always be set before the students move on to a new Unit.

Additional Reading Material
It is essential for the students to read as much as possible in their own time. The books set for extra-curricular reading should be simplified and well within their range. The following readers are suggested to accompany the Units in this book:
Units 1 and 2: As many titles as possible from Longman Simplified English Series.
Unit 3: As many titles as possible from Longman Bridge Series.

Additional Oral Practice
If additional oral practice is required, it may be obtained from the following:
The Carters of Greenwood (cineloops) Intermediate Level, published by Longman Group Limited.
Question and Answer Chapters 5 and 6, published by Longman Group Limited.

Additional Written Practice
If additional practice in writing is required, the following books may be used to accompany the Units in this course:
Précis
Unit 1: *A First Book in Comprehension, Précis and Composition* Chapter 4, Passages 61–70.
Unit 2: *A First Book in Comprehension, Précis and Composition* Chapter 4, Passages 71–70.
  Sixty Steps to Précis Part I, Passages 1–10.
Unit 3: *Sixty Steps to Précis* Part I, Passages 11–30.

Composition
Units 1–3: *Essay and Letter Writing*, Chapters 3 and 5.

Letter-writing
Units 1–3: *Essay and Letter Writing*, Chapter 4.

Future Work
If the student wishes to proceed further, he may go on to the following course which is designed to 'overlap' this one: *Fluency in English: An Integrated Course for Advanced Students.*

IF YOU CAN DO THIS TEST GO ON TO UNIT 1

Key Structures

A. Word Order.
Rewrite these sentences using the joining words in brackets:
1. My hotel room overlooked a court-yard. There was a fountain. There were several trees. (*in which . . . and*)
2. Uncle Charles looked everywhere for his glasses. He could not find them. (*Though*)
3. During Christmas, there was extra work at the post office. A great number of students were employed to help. (*so much . . . that*)
4. I don't want to see that film. It had poor reviews. (*because*)
5. Wages have gone up. Prices will rise. The cost of living will be higher than ever. (*Now that . . . and*)
6. The police searched everywhere. The missing boy could not be found. His dog could not be found. (*Although . . . neither . . . nor*)
7. James Sullivan will give a lecture at the local library next week. His book on the Antarctic was published recently. (*whose*)
8. Fares have increased. The railway company is still losing money. The employees have demanded higher wages. (*In spite of the fact that . . . because*)
9. He gave me a fright. I knocked the teapot over. (*such . . . that*)
10. The climbers reached the top of the mountain. They spent the night there. (*not only . . . but . . . as well*)

B. Composition.
Write two paragraphs in about 150 words using the ideas given below:
1. Circus act—a man was walking on a tight-rope—rode a one-wheel bicycle—carried two others on his shoulders—the crowd clapped his performance.
2. The man returned to give a repeat performance—tight-rope again—he did a hand-stand on the one-wheel bicycle—lost his balance—the crowd gasped—the man grabbed the tight-rope—he was still holding on to the bicycle—climbed on again and rode to the other side.

C. Verbs.
a What happened? What has happened? What has been happening?
Give the correct form of the verbs in brackets:
The mummy of an Egyptian woman who (die) in 800 B.C. just (have) an operation. As there (be) strange marks on the X-ray plates taken of the mummy, doctors (try) to find out whether the woman (die) of a rare disease. The only way to do this (be) to operate. The operation, which (last) for over four hours, (prove) to be very difficult. The doctors (remove) a section of the mummy and (send) it to a laboratory. They also (find) something which the X-ray plates not (show). The doctors not (decide) yet how the woman (die). They (fear) that the mummy would fall to pieces when they (cut) it open, but fortunately, this not (happen). The mummy successfully (survive) the operation.

b What happened? What was happening? What used to happen?
Give the correct form of the verbs in brackets. Use *would* in place of *used to* where possible:
I (travel) by air a great deal when I (be) a boy. My parents (live) in South America and I (fly) there from Europe in the holidays. An air-hostess (take) charge of me and

2

I never (have) an unpleasant experience. I am used to travelling by air and only on one occasion have I ever felt frightened. After taking off, we (fly) low over the city and slowly (gain) height, when the plane suddenly (turn) round and (fly) back to the airport. While we (wait) to land, an air-hostess (tell) us to keep calm, and to get off the plane quietly as soon as it had touched down.

c What will happen?
Give the correct form of the verbs in brackets:
Busmen have decided to go on strike next week. The strike is due to begin on Tuesday. No one knows how long it (last). The busmen have stated that the strike (continue) until general agreement (reach) about pay and working conditions. Most people believe that the strike (last) for a week. Many owners of private cars (offer) 'free rides' to people on their way to work. This (relieve) pressure on the trains to some extent. Meanwhile, a number of university students have volunteered to drive buses while the strike (last). All the young men are expert drivers, but before they (drive) any of the buses, they (have to) pass a special test.

d What will happen? What will be happening? What will have been happening?
Give the correct form of the verbs in brackets:
I have just received a letter from my old school informing me that my former head-master, Mr Reginald Page, (retire) next week. Pupils of the school, old and new, (send) him a present to mark the occasion. All those who have contributed towards the gift (sign) their names in a large album which (send) to the headmaster's home. We all (remember) Mr Page for his patience and understanding and for the kindly encourage-ment he gave us when we went so unwillingly to school. A great many former pupils (attend) a farewell dinner in his honour next Thursday. It is a curious coincidence that the day before his retirement, Mr Page (teach) for a total of forty years. After he (retire) he (devote) himself to gardening. For him, this (be) an entirely new hobby.

e What happened? What had happened? What had been happening?
Give the correct form of the verbs in brackets:
As the man tried to swing the speed-boat round, the steering-wheel came away in his hands. He (wave) desperately to his companion who (water ski) for the last fifteen minutes. Both men hardly (have) time to realize what was happening when they (throw) violently into the sea. The speed-boat (strike) a buoy, but it (continue) to move very quickly across the water. Both men just (begin) to swim towards the shore, when they (notice) with dismay that the speed-boat was moving in a circle. It now (come) towards them at tremendous speed. In less than a minute, it (roar) past them only a few feet away.

f Give the correct form of the verbs in brackets:
1. Captain Scott (find) that Amundsen (reach) the South Pole before him.
2. We just (move) to a new house but we (be) dissatisfied with it.
3. When I (meet) him two weeks ago, he (tell) me that he just (return) from the south of France.
4. Many new records (set up) in the next Olympic Games.
5. He always (go) for a walk every morning before his illness.
6. By next June, I (study) English for three years.
7. While the two thieves (argue) someone (steal) their car.

g Give the correct form of the verbs in brackets:
Though people have often laughed at stories told by seamen, it . . . now (know) that many 'monsters' which . . . at times (sight) are simply strange fish. Occasionally, unusual creatures (wash) to the shore, but they . . . rarely (catch) out at sea. Some time ago, however, a peculiar fish (catch) near Madagascar. A small fishing-boat (carry) miles out to sea by the powerful fish as it pulled on the line. When it . . . even-

tually (bring) to shore, it (find) to be over thirteen feet long. The fish, which . . . since (send) to a museum where it (examine) by a scientist, (call) an oarfish. Such creatures . . . rarely (see) alive by man as they live at a depth of six hundred feet.

h Write a report of this conversation as it might appear in a newspaper:
'At the time the murder was committed, I was travelling on the 8.0 o'clock train to London,' said the man.
'Do you always catch such an early train?' asked the inspector.
'Of course I do,' answered the man. 'I must be at work at 10.0 o'clock. My employer will confirm that I was there on time.'
'Would a later train get you to work on time?' asked the inspector.
'I suppose it would, but I never catch a later train.'
'At what time did you arrive at the station?'
'At ten to eight. I bought a paper and waited for the train.'
'And you didn't notice anything unusual?'
'Of course not.'

i If.
Give the correct form of the verbs in brackets:
1. If they (not bring) to the surface soon they may lose their lives.
2. If explosives are used, vibrations (cause) the roof of the mine to collapse.
3. If there had not been a hard layer of rock beneath the soil, they (complete) the job in a few hours.

j Give the correct form of the verbs in brackets:
I tried to wake up my wife by (ring) the door-bell, but she was fast asleep, so I got a ladder from the shed in the garden, put it against the wall, and began (climb) towards the bedroom window. I was almost there when a sarcastic voice below said, 'I don't think the windows need (clean) at this time of the night.' I looked down and nearly fell off the ladder when I saw a policeman. I immediately regretted (answer) in the way I did, but I said, 'I enjoy (clean) windows at night.'
'So do I,' answered the policeman in the same tone. 'Excuse my (interrupt) you. I hate (interrupt) a man when he's busy (work), but would you mind (come) with me to the station?'
'Well, I'd prefer (stay) here,' I said. 'You see, I've forgotten my key.'

D. Other Verbs.
a Supply the correct form of *have to* or *should* in these sentences:
1. I'm sorry I couldn't get here on time. I (. . . go) to the bank.
2. I (. . . go) to the dentist yesterday but I forgot all about it.
3. We (. . . begin) work at 9 o'clock but we never do.

b Write these sentences again using *have* with the verbs in italics:
1. 'I *shall deliver* the parcel,' said the shop-assistant.
2. Are you going *to clean* this suit?
3. When will you *dye* this jacket?

c Supply the correct form of *can* or *able to* in the following:
1. . . . you show me the way to the station please?
2. I gave him a few lessons and he . . . soon swim.
3. They . . . jump into the sea before the boat sank.
4. You . . . not leave this room until you get permission.

E. A and The.
Put in *a(n)* or *the* where necessary.
After reading . . . article entitled '. . . Cigarette Smoking and Your Health', I lit . . . cigarette to calm my nerves. I smoked with . . . concentration and . . . pleasure as I

4

was sure that this would be my last cigarette. For . . . whole week I did not smoke at all and during this time my wife suffered terribly. I had all . . . usual symptoms of someone giving up . . . smoking: . . . bad temper and . . . enormous appetite. My friends kept on offering me . . . cigarettes and . . . cigars. They made no effort to hide their amusement whenever I produced . . . packet of . . . sweets from my pocket.

F. Supply the missing words in the following:
Perhaps the . . . extraordinary building of the nineteenth century was The Crystal Palace which was built in Hyde Park for the Great Exhibition of 1851. The Crystal Palace was different . . . all other buildings . . . the world, for it was made of iron and glass. It was one of the . . . (big) buildings . . . all time and a . . . of people from . . . countries came to see it. A great . . . goods were sent to the exhibition from various parts of the world. There was also a great . . . of machinery on display.

G. Supply the missing words in these sentences:
  1. There will be a dance tonight . . . the Green Park Hotel.
  2. The players . . . our team are all . . . red shirts.
  3. He returned . . . England . . . August 10th.
  4. I'll meet you . . . the corner . . . Wednesday.
  5. I always feel tired . . . the end of the day.
  6. As soon as he got . . . the taxi, he asked the driver to take him . . . the station.
  7. We'll go for a walk . . . the afternoon.
  8. He's incapable . . . controlling the class.
  9. He is not interested . . . anything outside his work.
  10. I don't want to be involved . . . this unpleasant affair.
  11. He failed . . . his attempt to reach the top of the mountain.
  12. The surgeon decided to operate . . . the patient.
  13. I am not satisfied . . . your explanation.
  14. I think someone is knocking . . . the door.
  15. His debts amount . . . £500.

Special Difficulties

a Words Often Confused.
Choose the correct words in the following sentences:
  1. You can divide this apple (among) (between) the two of you.
  2. He arrived late as (usually) (usual).
  3. Mr Simpson has been appointed (director) (headmaster) of the school.
  4. What shall we do with this old (clothing) (clothes)?
  5. I always wear out (clothes) (cloths) quickly.
  6. His instructions were not very (clear) (clean).
  7. You should wait until the road is (clear) (clean) before crossing.
  8. Did you (wash) (wash up) your hands?
  9. I don't feel in the (mood) (temper) for a walk.
  10. Whatever you do, don't lose your (temper) (mood).
  11. This coffee is (too) (enough) hot for me to drink.
  12. The questions were (fairly) (enough) difficult, but I managed to answer them.
  13. He is (enough old) (old enough) to know what is right.
  14. You should use (petrol) (benzine) to get those stains off.

b Write sentences using each of the following:
  1. Get up, get over, get away, get out.
  2. Keep off, keep out, keep in, keep up.

5

3. Take in, take up, take off, take away.
4. Run into, run out of, run away, run after.
5. Make up, make for, make out, make up for.

c Write sentences using the following:
1. Turn yellow. 2. Go sour. 3. Grow dark. 4. Fall ill. 5. Come true. 6. Get angry.

d Complete the following sentences using *so . . . I* or *neither . . . I*.
1. She reads a lot and . . .
2. You shouldn't work so hard and . . .
3. You are mistaken and . . .
4. You will regret it and . . .
5. Tom telephoned him yesterday and . . .
6. She hasn't been well and . . .

Unit 1

INSTRUCTIONS TO THE STUDENT

Before you begin each exercise, read these instructions carefully. Read them *each time* you begin a new piece. They are very important.

How to Work—Comprehension and Précis

Unit 1 contains twenty passages. You will be asked to write a summary of a part of each piece. In Unit 4 of *Practice and Progress* you were given the main points and asked to join them up. Connections were provided in the text. Now you will be expected to find the main points yourself and supply your own connections. The Comprehension questions which are given should be answered *in note form*. Your notes should be very brief.

1. Read the passage two or three times. Make sure you understand it.
2. Read the instructions which will tell you where your précis should begin and end, and exactly what you will have to do.
3. Read again the part of the passage you will have to summarize.
4. Answer each of the Comprehension questions in note form to get your points.
5. You will find brackets at the side of the questions. These show you how the answers might be joined to form sentences, but you will have to use your own joining words. You may ignore the brackets if you wish to join the points in your own way.
6. When joining your points, you may refer to the passage if necessary, but try to use *your own words* as far as possible. Your answer should be in one paragraph.
7. Read through your work and correct your mistakes.
8. At the end of your précis, write the number of words that you have used. Remember that words like 'the' 'a' etc. count as single words. Words which are joined by a hyphen (e.g. 'living-room') also count as single words. You may write fewer than 80 words, but you must not go over the word limit.

Example

Work through this example carefully and then try to do the exercises in Unit 1 in the same way.

Silent Enemies

Few countries will admit officially that they employ spies. However, from time to time, a spy is caught and the public sometimes gets a glimpse of what is going on behind the political scenes. Spies are rarely shot these days. They are frequently tried and imprisoned. If a spy is important enough, he is sometimes
5 handed back to an enemy country in exchange for an equally important spy whom the enemy have caught. Few people have the opportunity to witness such exchanges, for they are carried out in secret.
   One cold winter morning on December 17th last year, a small blue car stopped on a bridge in a provincial town in northern Germany. Three men dressed in
10 heavy black coats got out and stood on the bridge. While they waited there, they kept on looking over the side. Fifteen minutes later, a motor-boat sailed past and drew up by the river-bank. Three men got out of the boat and looked up at the bridge. The men on the bridge silently walked down the stone steps leading to the river-bank. No words were spoken when they met the men from the boat.
15 After a while, the motor-boat moved off and three men returned to the bridge. Now, only two of them were wearing black coats. The third was dressed in a light

8

grey jacket. Anyone who had been watching the scene might not have realized that two master spies had been exchanged on that cold winter morning.

Comprehension and Précis

In not more than 80 words describe what happened on the morning of December 17th from the time a small blue car stopped on a bridge. Do not include anything that is not in the last paragraph.

Answer these questions in note form to get your points:

1. Did the car stop or not?
2. How many men got out?
3. How were they dressed?
4. Where did they stand?
5. Where did they keep looking?
6. Did a motor-boat appear or not?
7. Where did it stop?
8. Where did the men go?
9. Why did they go to the river-bank?
10. Did the boat move off or not?
11. Who accompanied the men in black coats?
12. How was he dressed?
13. Did they return to the bridge or not?
14. Had two master spies been exchanged or not?

A Possible Answer

Points

1. Car stopped.
2. Three men got out.
3. Black coats.
4. Stood—bridge.
5. Looked over side.
6. Motor-boat appeared.
7. Stopped—river-bank.
8. Men—down steps.
9. Met boat.
10. Boat moved off.
11. Man accompanied by others.
12. Grey jacket.
13. Returned—bridge.
14. Spies exchanged.

Précis

After the car stopped, three men *in* black coats got out *and* stood on the bridge. They kept looking over the side *until* a motor-boat appeared. *When* it stopped by the river-bank, the men on the bridge silently climbed down the stone steps *to* meet the men from the boat. *As soon as* the boat moved off, a man *in* a grey jacket accompanied by two men in black coats returned to the bridge. Two master spies had been exchanged.

(80 words.)

Vocabulary

In this exercise, you will be asked to explain words and phrases. You may use a phrase to explain a word if necessary. Try to find another word to replace the word or phrase in the passage.

Example

Study the example below to find out how this is done:

Give another word or phrase to replace the following words as they are used in the passage: employ (l. 1); from time to time (ll. 1–2); gets a glimpse (l. 2); rarely (l. 3); frequently (ll. 3–4); handed (l. 5); witness (l. 6).

A Possible Answer

employ: provide work for.
from time to time: now and again.
gets a glimpse of: is able to see briefly.
rarely: seldom.
frequently: often.
handed: given.
witness: see.

Composition

Composition exercises are based on ideas suggested by each passage. You will be given two types of composition exercise:

1. You will be asked to expand a number of uncompleted sentences so that you write a paragraph of about 150 words. You are free to expand each sentence *in any way you please* providing that what you write fits in logically with the rest of the passage.
2. You will be given a full plan which contains notes for an essay in three paragraphs: an Introduction, Development, and Conclusion. You should write a composition of about 200 words based on these notes. You are quite free to add ideas of your own or ignore ideas that are to be found in the plan.

Examples

Work through these examples carefully and then try to do the composition exercises in Unit 1 in the same way.

1. Composition

Write an imaginary account of how one of the spies mentioned in the passage was caught. Expand the following into a paragraph of about 150 words.

Colonel Hepworth had been employed ... In time, he rose to the position of ... Soon after his appointment ... No one suspected the Colonel until ... Even then, it was impossible to ... because ... However, Hepworth was ... The police noticed that he ... and ... One evening, they ... and found him ... After Hepworth was ... it was learnt that ... He had ...   (54 words).

A Possible Answer

Colonel Hepworth had been employed *in the War Office for years.* In time, he rose to the position of *Chief Private Secretary to the Minister.* Soon after his appointment, *important people in the War Office began complaining that many State secrets had become known to the enemy.* No one suspected the Colonel until *a stranger telephoned the police and claimed that he had received large sums of money from Hepworth to obtain information about air-bases.* Even then, it was impossible to *make any arrest* because *nothing could be proved against him.* However, Hepworth was *watched closely.* The police noticed that he *often stayed behind in the evenings* and *was often the last person to leave the War Office.* One evening, they *suddenly burst into his room* and found him *holding a pile of secret documents.* After Hepworth was *arrested,* it was learnt that *his real name was Christopher Bulin.* He had *become famous for his work as a spy during the war.*   (About 160 words.)

Now here is the same question with a different set of facts and different presentation:

2. Composition

In about 200 words, write an imaginary account of how one of the spies mentioned in the passage was caught. Use the ideas given below. Do not write more than three paragraphs.
Title: The Spy.
Introduction: Clerk—War Office—trusted.
Development: Expensive car—large sums of money to spend—flat—parties—money 'inherited'—police checked story—false—flat watched—visited by members of Uranian Embassy.
Conclusion: Police entered flat—documents—transmitter—'clerk' confessed.

A Possible Answer

The Spy

Andrew Whibley worked as a clerk in the War Office. Though he did not have an important position, he was trusted by everybody.

One day, Whibley arrived at his office in a very expensive car. Although his salary was small, he appeared to have large sums of money to spend. He rented an expensive flat and gave parties for many of his friends. When he was asked how he had suddenly got so much money to spend, Whibley explained that he had inherited a large fortune from an aunt who had died a few months before. However, War Office officials were suspicious and they asked the police to check Whibley's story. The police soon discovered that Whibley had not been telling the truth. They kept a close watch on his flat and noticed that members of the Uranian Embassy often went there.

The police entered Whibley's flat when he was out and discovered copies of several secret documents and a radio transmitter which had been hidden inside a piano. After Whibley was arrested, he confessed that he had been receiving large sums of money from the Uranian Embassy to obtain official secrets.   (About 200 words).

Letter-writing

Follow the instructions given under each passage.

Key Structures and Special Difficulties

When you finish your Letter-writing exercise, go on to the language exercises that follow. In this Unit, you will be given the opportunity to revise briefly each one of the **Key Structures** dealt with in *Practice and Progress*. You may refer to *Practice and Progress* if you have forgotten anything. New **Special Difficulties** are introduced after the Key Structures. The work you do in grammar is based on material contained in the passages. Refer to the passages frequently. They will help you to understand the grammar and to do the exercises.

1 A Puma at Large

Pumas are large, cat-like animals which are found in America. When reports came into London Zoo that a wild puma had been spotted forty-five miles south of London, they were not taken seriously. However, as the evidence began to accumulate, experts from the Zoo felt obliged to investigate, for the descriptions given by people who claimed to have seen the puma were extraordinarily similar.

evidence began to accumulate

The hunt for the puma began in a small village where a woman picking blackberries saw 'a large cat' only five yards away from her. It immediately ran away when she saw it, and experts confirmed that a puma will not attack a human being unless it is cornered. The search proved difficult, for the puma was often observed at one place in the morning and at another place twenty miles away in the evening. Wherever it went, it left behind it a trail of dead deer and small animals like rabbits. Paw prints were seen in a number of places and puma fur was found clinging to bushes. Several people complained of 'cat-like noises' at night and a business-man on a fishing trip saw the puma up a tree. The experts were now fully convinced that the animal *was* a puma, but where had it come from? As no pumas had been reported missing from any zoo in the country, this one must have been in the possession of a private collector and somehow managed to escape. The hunt went on for several weeks, but the puma was not caught. It is disturbing to think that a dangerous wild animal is still at large in the quiet countryside.

Comprehension and Précis

In not more than 80 words describe how experts came to the conclusion that the animal seen by many people really was a puma. Do not include anything that is not in the passage.

Answer these questions in note form to get your points:

1. What sort of reports were received by London Zoo?
2. Were the reports similar in nature or not?
3. Who saw it first?
4. Did it stay in one place, or did it move from place to place?
5. What did it leave behind it?
6. Were paw-prints and puma fur found as well or not?
7. What was heard at night?
8. Was the animal seen up a tree or not?
9. Were experts now sure that the animal really was a puma or not?

Vocabulary

Give another word or phrase to replace the following words as they are used in the passage: spotted (l. 4); accumulate (l. 7); obliged to (l. 8); claimed (l. 9); extraordinarily similar (ll. 10–11); immediately (l. 15); convinced (l. 24).

Composition

Describe the occasion when the woman picking blackberries saw the puma. Expand the following into a paragraph of about 150 words.
Mrs Stone had spent the whole morning . . . It was nearly lunch time, so she decided . . . She was just . . . when she heard a noise in . . . Then she saw an animal which . . . She knew it was not a cat because . . . The animal suddenly . . . and she thought it was going to . . . She dropped her basket and . . . Hearing the sound, the animal . . . after which, Mrs Stone . . . and ran all the way home. She told her neighbours that . . . but they did not believe her. She also telephoned the police but they . . .   (86 words.)

Letter-writing

On a full page, show the exact position of each of the following:
The address and date; the beginning of the letter; the Introduction; the Purpose; the Conclusion; the letter-ending; the signature; the postscript. Supply all necessary full stops and commas.

Key Structures

Simple, Compound and Complex Statements. (1 KS 186)

Exercise
Underline all the joining words in the passage. Note carefully how simple statements have been joined to make compound or complex statements.

Special Difficulties

Where had it come from? (l. 24)

Instead of saying:	*It is better to say:*
About whom are you talking?	Who(m) are you talking about?
That is the film about which I told you.	That is the film I told you about. Compare 1 SD 78.

Exercises
A. Complete these sentences by adding a suitable word to the end of each one:
1. What are you looking . . . ?
2. Where is your mother going . . . ?
3. Whom has the letter been sent . . . ?
4. This is the house I was born . . .
5. What does your decision depend . . . ?

B. Write these sentences again changing the position of the words in italics. Where possible, omit the words *whom* or *which*.
1. He is the man *about* whom we have heard so much.
2. The shelf *on* which you put those books has collapsed.
3. *From* whom did you receive a letter?
4. This is the road *by* which we came.
5. Where is the pencil *with* which you were playing?

2 Thirteen Equals One

Our vicar is always raising money for one cause or another, but he has never managed to get enough money to have the church clock repaired. The big clock
5 which used to strike the hours day and night was damaged during the war and has been silent ever since.

our vicar woke up with a start

One night, however, our vicar woke up with a start: the clock was striking the
10 hours! Looking at his watch, he saw that it was one o'clock, but the bell struck thirteen times before it stopped. Armed with a torch, the vicar went up into the clock tower to see what was going on. In
15 the torchlight, he caught sight of a figure whom he immediately recognized as Bill Wilkins, our local grocer.

'Whatever are you doing up here Bill?' asked the vicar in surprise.

'I'm trying to repair the bell,' answered Bill. 'I've been coming up here night
20 after night for weeks now. You see, I was hoping to give you a surprise.'

'You certainly did give me a surprise!' said the vicar. 'You've probably woken up everyone in the village as well. Still, I'm glad the bell is working again.'

'That's the trouble, vicar,' answered Bill. 'It's working all right, but I'm
25 afraid that at one o'clock it will strike thirteen times and there's nothing I can do about it.'

'We'll get used to that Bill,' said the vicar. 'Thirteen is not as good as one, but it's better than nothing. Now let's go downstairs and have a cup of tea.'

Comprehension and Précis

In not more than 80 words describe what happened from the moment the vicar woke up. Do not include anything that is not in the passage.
Answer these questions in note form to get your points:

1. What woke the vicar up?
2. What was the time?
3. How many times did the clock strike?
4. Where did the vicar go?
5. What did he take with him?
6. Whom did he see in the clock tower?
7. What did Bill Wilkins say he was trying to do?
8. Had Bill Wilkins succeeded in repairing the clock or not?
9. Was the vicar pleased or angry?
10. What did he offer the grocer?

Vocabulary

Give another word or phrase to replace the following words as they are used in the passage: vicar (l. 1); repaired (l. 4); damaged (l. 6); silent (l. 7); with a start (l. 9); caught sight of (l. 15).

Composition

Write a composition of about 200 words using the ideas given below:
Title : A Sticky Business.
Introduction : A small village—the church clock suddenly stopped—no one could explain why.
Development : The vicar climbed into the clock tower—found that the clock had been invaded by bees—full of honey and wax.
Conclusion : A bee-keeper was called—removed the queen bee—the other bees followed —the clock was cleaned—working again.

Letter-writing

Write six phrases which could be used to begin letters to friends.

Key Structures

What is happening? What always happens? (1 KS 188)
Note that with the word *always* we can sometimes say:
Our vicar is always raising money. (l. 1)
He is always getting into trouble.
She is always writing letters.

Exercise
Underline the verbs in the passage that tell us *what is happening* now. Note how they have been used.

Special Difficulties

Phrases with In. Compare 1 SD 108, 200.
Study these examples:
'Whatever are you doing up here Bill?' asked the vicar *in surprise*. (l. 18)
Please write *in ink*, not *in pencil*.
We have a great deal *in common*.
The swimmer seemed to be *in difficulty*, but he managed to reach the shore *in the end*.
I didn't feel well so I spent the day *in bed*.
We have received fifty applications *in all*.
The thieves were disturbed and left *in a hurry*.
I can't borrow any more money; I'm already *in debt*.
Mary's *in love* with a sailor.
There wasn't a person *in sight*.
He didn't realize that he was *in danger*.
The little boy was *in tears*.

Exercise
Use a phrase with *in* in place of the words in italics.
1. I left home *very quickly* so as not to miss the train.
2. I suppose I shall finish this *eventually*.
3. In the early morning there was not a person *to be seen*.
4. Shall I write *with a pen* or *with a pencil*?
5. They haven't many interests *which they share*.
6. Why is that little girl *crying*?

3   An Unknown Goddess

Some time ago, an interesting discovery was made by archaeologists on the Aegean island of Kea. An American team explored a temple which stands in an
5 ancient city on the promontory of Ayia Irini. The city at one time must have been prosperous, for it enjoyed a high level of civilization. Houses—often three storeys high—were built of stone. They
10 had large rooms with beautifully decorated walls. The city was even equipped with a drainage system, for a great many clay pipes were found beneath the narrow streets.

a very modern-looking woman

15   The temple which the archaeologists explored was used as a place of worship from the fifteenth century B.C. until Roman times. In the most sacred room of the temple, clay fragments of fifteen statues were found. Each of these represented a goddess and had, at one time, been painted. The body of one statue
20 was found among remains dating from the fifteenth century B.C. Its missing head happened to be among remains of the fifth century B.C. This head must have been found in Classical times and carefully preserved. It was very old and precious even then. When the archaeologists reconstructed the fragments, they were amazed to find that the goddess turned out to be a very modern-looking
25 woman. She stood three feet high and her hands rested on her hips. She was wearing a full-length skirt which swept the ground. Despite her great age, she was very graceful indeed, but, so far, the archaeologists have been unable to discover her identity.

Comprehension and Précis

In not more than 80 words describe what archaeologists discovered in an ancient temple on the island of Kea. Do not include anything that is not in the last paragraph.
Answer these questions in note form to get your points:
  1. Where did the archaeologists find clay fragments?
  2. What did they represent?
  3. Had they once been painted or not?
  4. Where was the body of one statue found?
  5. Where was its head found?
  6. Were the fragments reconstructed or not?
  7. How tall did the goddess turn out to be?
  8. Where did her hands rest?
  9. What was she wearing?
  10. Is her identity known or not?

Vocabulary

Give another word or phrase to replace the following words as they are used in the passage: explored (ll. 3–4); ancient (l. 5); prosperous (l. 7); storeys (l. 9); beneath (l. 13); fragments (l. 18); remains (l. 20).

Composition

Write an imaginary account of how the archaeologists explored the sacred room of the ancient temple. Expand the following into a paragraph of about 150 words.

After walking round the ancient city, the archaeologists ... This temple ... On entering the sacred room, the archaeologists ... After this, workmen began digging and soon discovered ... They also found ... The archaeologists carefully ... They were astonished to find that ... The goddess was ... She ... Although the archaeologists ... they were unable to find out her name.   (52 words)

Letter-writing

Write six phrases which could be used to end letters to friends.

Key Structures

What happened? (1 KS 190)

Exercise

Suppose that each of the following verbs were used to describe *what happened* yesterday. What would be their correct form?

Yesterday I ... leave, lay, lie, choose, raise, rise, beat, bite, catch, hear, sing, think, show, run, lose, begin, fall, feel.

Special Difficulties

Words Often Misused and Confused.

a Happen. Study these examples:

Its missing head *happened to be* among remains of the fifth century B.C. (By chance.) (ll. 20–21)

I *happened to find* the ticket in my pocket. (By chance.)

It happened that I found the ticket in my pocket. (By chance.)

I couldn't find out what had *happened*. (What had taken place.)

Exercises

a Complete the following making a sentence out of each:

1. She happened ...
2. It happened ...
3. Tell me what ...
4. If you happen ...

b Storey and Story. Study these examples:

Houses—often three storeys high—were built of stone. (ll. 8–9)

c Worship and Warship. Study these examples:

The temple ... was used as a place of worship. (ll. 15–16)

The *Arethusa* used to be a warship.

Exercise

Use the words storey, story, worship, and warship in sentences of your own.

4 The Double Life of Alfred Bloggs

These days, people who do manual work often receive far more money than clerks who work in offices. People who work in offices are frequently referred to as 'white
5 collar workers' for the simple reason that they usually wear a collar and tie to go to work. Such is human nature, that a great many people are often willing to sacrifice higher pay for the privilege of becoming
10 white collar workers. This can give rise to curious situations, as it did in the case of Alfred Bloggs who worked as a dustman for the Ellesmere Corporation.

. . . he then changed

When he got married, Alf was too
15 embarrassed to say anything to his wife about his job. He simply told her that he worked for the Corporation. Every morning, he left home dressed in a fine black suit. He then changed into overalls and spent the next eight hours as a dustman. Before returning home at night, he took a shower and changed back into his
20 suit. Alf did this for over two years and his fellow dustmen kept his secret. Alf's wife has never discovered that she married a dustman and she never will, for Alf has just found another job. He will soon be working in an office as a junior clerk. He will be earning only half as much as he used to, but he feels that his rise in status is well worth the loss of money. From now on, he will wear a suit
25 all day and others will call him 'Mr Bloggs', not 'Alf'.

Comprehension and Précis

In not more than 80 words describe how Alfred Bloggs prevented his wife from finding out that he worked as a dustman. Do not include anything that is not in the last paragraph.
Answer these questions in note form to get your points:
1. What did Alfred Bloggs tell his wife when they got married?]
2. How did he dress each morning before he left home?
3. Did he change into overalls or not?
4. How did he spend the day?
5. What did he do before going home at night?
6. For how long did this last?
7. Did his fellow dustmen keep his secret or not?
8. Will his wife ever learn the truth?
9. Where will her husband be working in future?

Vocabulary

Give another word or phrase to replace the following words as they are used in the passage: receive (l. 2); sacrifice (l. 8); privilege (l. 9); curious (l. 11); embarrassed (l. 15); discovered (l. 21); status (l. 24).

Composition

Write a composition of about 200 words using the ideas given below. Do not write more than three paragraphs.

Title: Nearly Caught.

Introduction: Alf and three other dustmen were collecting rubbish—arrived at Mrs Frost's house.

Development: Alf's wife was visiting Mrs Frost at the time—Alf was just getting out of the dustcart—saw his wife leaving Mrs Frost's house—hid in dustcart—dustmen helped him—his wife talked to Mrs Frost on the doorstep.

Conclusion: The dustcart drove away just as Mrs Bloggs came towards it.

Letter-writing

Write a letter of about 80 words to an acquaintance whom you do not know very well asking him to lend you a book you know he possesses. Supply a suitable Introduction and Conclusion.

Use the following ideas to write your *Purpose*: ask for loan of book—its title—why you want it—how long you will keep it—you will take good care of it.

Key Structures

What has happened? What has been happening? (1 KS 192)

Exercises

A. Find two verbs in the passage which tell us *what has happened* and note how they have been used.

B. Write sentences using each of the following words or phrases: since last April; up till now; just; ever; yet.

Special Difficulties

Alf was too embarrassed to say anything to his wife. (ll. 14–15) Compare 1 SD 18.

a Study these examples:

He explained the difficulty *to me*.

I described the scene *to my wife*.

He said nothing *to me* about it.

Did you suggest this idea *to him?* .

I confided the secret *to my sister*.

Exercises

a Write sentences using the following combinations of words:

1. describe/film/aunt.   2. say/nothing/her.   3. explain/the position/me.   4. propose/idea/us.

b Words Often Misused: Worth.

Study these examples:

His rise in status is well worth the loss of money. (ll. 23–24)

That film is not worth seeing. Compare 1 KS 166a.

Exercise

Choose the correct words in the following:

1. (Is) (Does) it worth five pounds?
2. Is this worth (buying) (to buy)?
3. Your car (does) (is) not worth £500.
4. I don't think it is worth (to go) (going) to all that trouble.

19

5 The Facts

Editors of newspapers and magazines often go to extremes to provide their readers with unimportant facts and statistics. Last year a journalist had been
5 instructed by a well-known magazine to write an article on the president's palace in a new African republic. When the article arrived, the editor read the first sentence and then refused to publish it.
10 The article began: 'Hundreds of steps lead to the high wall which surrounds the president's palace.' The editor at once sent the journalist a telegram instructing him to find out the exact number of steps
15 and the height of the wall.

. . . to obtain these important facts

The journalist immediately set out to obtain these important facts, but he took a long time to send them. Meanwhile, the editor was getting impatient, for the magazine would soon go to press. He sent the journalist two urgent telegrams, but received no reply. He sent yet
20 another telegram informing the journalist that if he did not reply soon he would be fired. When the journalist again failed to reply, the editor reluctantly published the article as it had originally been written. A week later, the editor at last received a telegram from the journalist. Not only had the poor man been arrested, but he had been sent to prison as well. However, he had at last been
25 allowed to send a cable in which he informed the editor that he had been arrested while counting the 1084 steps leading to the 15 foot wall which surrounded the president's palace.

Comprehension and Précis

In not more than 80 words describe what happened from the time the journalist set out to get the facts. Do not include anything that is not in the last paragraph.
Answer these questions in note form to get your points:
1. Did the journalist immediately set out to get the facts after receiving instructions from his editor or not?
2. Did he send them at once or not?
3. Was the editor getting impatient or not?
4. How many telegrams did the editor send?
5. What did the editor threaten to do?
6. Was the last telegram answered or not?
7. Was the article omitted from the magazine, or was it printed in its original form?
8. When did the journalist send a telegram?
9. Why had he been imprisoned?

Vocabulary

Give another word or phrase to replace the following words as they are used in the passage: journalist (l. 4); instructed (l. 5); well-known (l. 5); publish (l. 9); surrounds (l. 11); fired (l. 21); reluctantly (l. 21).

Composition

Describe how the journalist was arrested and what happened afterwards. Expand the following into a paragraph of about 150 words.

The journalist counted the number of steps as he . . . On arriving outside the main gate, he . . . He then . . . in order to measure the wall. While he was busy measuring the wall, a policeman . . . Though the journalist . . . , the policeman refused to believe him. He was arrested and sent to prison because the police thought that . . . When the journalist . . . he made things worse for himself. This proved to the police that . . .

(69 words)

Letter-writing

Write a letter of about 80 words to a friend who has recently got married. You read about the wedding in your local paper. Supply a suitable Introduction and Conclusion. Use the following ideas to write the *Purpose*: Surprise and pleasure at seeing newspaper report—glad to hear that he and his wife will be staying in your neighbourhood —hope to see them soon.

Key Structures

A, The and Some. (1 KS 196)

Exercises

A. Underline the words *a(n)* and *the* in the passage and note how they have been used.

B. Write sentences using the following words and phrases:
1. Hudson river. 2. information. 3. cinema. 4. industry. 5. flour and milk.
6. newspaper.

Special Difficulties

Not only had the poor man been arrested . . . (ll. 23–24)
Study these pairs of sentences:

I have never seen so many people.
Never have I seen so many people.

I had hardly finished speaking when the door opened.
Hardly had I finished speaking when the door opened. (Compare 1 SD 98a)

He little realizes the danger he is in.
Little does he realize the danger he is in.

Exercise

Write these sentences again beginning each one with the words in italics:
1. He has *not only* made this mistake before but he will make it again.
2. I realized what was happening *only then*.
3. I will *never* trust him again.
4. You *seldom* find traffic wardens who are kind and helpful.

6 Smash and Grab

Break into many pieces. — *to take quickly (snatch)*

costly

The expensive shops in a famous arcade *— a group of / shop*
near Piccadilly were just opening. At this
time of the morning, the arcade was almost
empty. Mr Taylor, the owner of a jewel-
5 lery shop was admiring a new window
display. Two of his assistants *helper* had been
working busily since 8 o'clock and had
only just finished. Diamond necklaces
and rings had been beautifully arranged
10 on a background of black velvet. After
gazing at the display for several minutes,
Mr Taylor went back into his shop.
   The silence was suddenly broken when
a large car, with its headlights on and its
15 horn blaring, roared down the arcade. It
came to a stop outside the jeweller's. One
man stayed at the wheel while two others with black stockings over their faces
jumped out and smashed the window of the shop with iron bars. While this was
going on, Mr Taylor was upstairs. He and his staff began throwing furniture out
20 of the window. Chairs and tables went flying into the arcade. One of the thieves
was struck by a heavy statue, but he was too busy helping himself to diamonds
to notice any pain. The raid was all over in three minutes, for the men scrambled
back into the car and it moved off at a fantastic speed. Just as it was leaving,
Mr Taylor rushed out and ran after it throwing ashtrays and vases, but it was
25 impossible to stop the thieves. They had got away with thousands of pounds
worth of diamonds.

JEWELLER

too busy to notice any pain

Comprehension and Précis

Write an account of the smash and grab raid *in not more than 80 words*. Do not include
anything that is not in the last paragraph.
Answer these questions in note form to get your points:
1. Did a large car enter an arcade near Piccadilly or not?
2. Where did it stop?
3. How many thieves got out of the car?
4. Did they smash the window or not?
5. Where was the owner of the shop?
6. What did he and his staff throw at the thieves?
7. Did they hit any of the thieves or not?
8. How long did the raid last?
9. Did the thieves drive away or not?
10. Did the owner run after the car or did he stay in the shop?
11. What did he throw at the car?
12. Did the thieves get away or were they caught?
13. What had they stolen?

Vocabulary

Give another word or phrase to replace the following words as they are used in the
passage: expensive (l. 1); almost (l. 3); assistants (l. 6); gazing (l. 11); several (l. 11);
stayed (l. 17); smashed (l. 18).

Composition

In not more than 200 words continue the above passage using the ideas given below. Do not write more than three paragraphs.

Title: They Got Away.

Introduction: The thieves' car joined the traffic—Mr Taylor took a taxi—followed the thieves' car.

Development: A mad chase through the streets—the thieves' car hit another car—did not stop—the police chased both taxi and thieves—Mr Taylor's taxi stopped at traffic lights—the thieves got away—the taxi-driver was stopped by the police—he had been speeding—Mr Taylor explained the situation.

Conclusion: The thieves' car was found ten minutes later—side street—abandoned—the thieves escaped on foot.

Letter-writing

Suppose that you had witnessed an incident similar to the one described in the passage. Write a letter of about 80 words to a friend describing what you saw. Supply a suitable Introduction and Conclusion. Use the following ideas to write the *Purpose*: Tuesday morning—busy street—a man smashed the window of an antique shop—chased by passers-by—you joined in—the man was caught.

Key Structures

What happened? What was happening? (1 KS 198)

Exercises

A. Underline the verbs in the passage which tell us *what happened* and *what was happening*. Note how they have been used.

B. Write sentences using the following words and phrases: just as; used to; while.

Special Difficulties

Word Building.
Study these sentences:
It was possible to stop the thieves.
It was impossible to stop the thieves. (ll. 24–25)
Note how the opposite of 'possible' has been formed. We can add *dis, in, im, un, il* or *ir* to certain words to make opposites.

Exercise
Write these sentences again giving the correct opposites of the words in italics:
1. He was extremely *polite*.
2. I *agree* with you.
3. His handwriting is quite *legible*.
4. This report is *accurate*.
5. Have you *locked* the door?
6. Have you learnt these *regular* verbs?

7 Crazy

Children often have far more sense than
their elders. This simple truth was
demonstrated rather dramatically during
a civil defence exercise in a small town in
5 Canada. Most of the inhabitants were
asked to take part in the exercise during
which they had to pretend that their city
had been bombed. Air-raid warnings
were sounded and thousands of people
10 went into special air-raid shelters. Doctors
and nurses remained above ground while
police patrolled the streets in case anyone
tried to leave the shelters too soon.

*. . . to make the injuries
look realistic*

The police did not have much to do
15 because the citizens took the exercise
seriously. They stayed underground for
twenty minutes and waited for the siren to sound again. On leaving the air-raid
shelters, they saw that doctors and nurses were busy. A great many people had
volunteered to act as casualties. Theatrical make-up and artificial blood had
20 been used to make the injuries look realistic. A lot of people were lying 'dead'
in the streets. The living helped to carry the dead and wounded to special
stations. A child of six was brought in by two adults. The child was supposed to
be dead. With theatrical make-up on his face, he looked as if he had died of
shock. Some people were so moved by the sight that they began to cry. However,
25 the child suddenly sat up and a doctor asked him to comment on his death.
The child looked around for a moment and said, 'I think they're all crazy!'

Comprehension and Précis

In not more than 80 words describe the scene after the people left the air-raid shelters.
Do not include anything that is not in the last paragraph.
Answer these questions in note form to get your points:
1. Why were doctors and nurses busy during the civil defence exercise?
2. Were there many 'casualties'?
3. Did their injuries look realistic?
4. Where did the living carry the dead and wounded?
5. How many adults brought in a six-year old child?
6. What had the child 'died' of?
7. Were some people moved by the sight or not?
8. What did the child suddenly do?
9. What did the doctor ask him?
10. What was the child's opinion?

Vocabulary

Give another word or phrase to replace the following words as they are used in the
passage: demonstrated (l. 3); inhabitants (l. 5); pretend (l. 7); remained (l. 11); patrolled
(l. 12); volunteered (l. 19); artificial (l. 19).

Composition

Describe what happened when the air-raid warning sounded.
Expand the following into a paragraph of about 150 words.
Early that morning, people were informed on the radio that . . . However, the air-raid warning took everyone by surprise because . . . People immediately stopped whatever they were doing and . . . The streets were soon full of thousands of people who . . . Only one man objected to . . . A policeman tried to argue with him but . . . The man said that . . . and that the end of the world had come. The policeman . . . and conducted him to a shelter. In a short time, the streets . . . The city was . . . and only the wailing of the siren could be heard.   (90 words)

Letter-writing

Write a letter of about 80 words to a friend thanking him for his hospitality. Supply a suitable Introduction and Conclusion. Use the following ideas to write the *Purpose*: the pleasure of seeing your friend again—his kindness during your stay—things about the visit you will remember for a long time—hope you can return this hospitality one day.

Key Structures

Children often have far more sense than their elders. (1 KS 200)

Exercises
A. Note how the following have been used in the passage: more . . . than (l. 1); most (l. 5); much (l. 14); a great many (l. 18); a lot of (l. 20).

B. Write sentences using the following words and phrases: interesting than; a little; a few; a great deal of.

Special Difficulties

Suppose.
Study these examples:
I suppose he must be ill. (I think that . . .)
Suppose he's not at home. What shall I do then? (Let's assume . . .)
He is supposed to arrive at six o'clock. (He ought to . . .) (Compare 1 KS 160b)
The child was supposed to be dead. (ll. 22–23)
He was supposed to arrive last night.
He was supposed to have told me about it.

Exercise
Supply the correct form of *suppose* in the following sentences:
1. You . . . (go) to the doctor yesterday.
2. . . . he fails to arrive. What will you do then?
3. He . . . (finish) at 5 o'clock, but he never does.
4. This is an easy question. I . . . you know the answer.
5. Can you tell us what we are . . . to do?

8   A Famous Monastery

The Great St Bernard Pass connects
Switzerland to Italy. At 2470 metres, it is
the highest mountain pass in Europe.
The famous monastery of St Bernard,
5 which was founded in the eleventh century, lies about a mile away. For hundreds of years, St Bernard dogs have
saved the lives of travellers crossing the
dangerous Pass. These friendly dogs,
10 which were first brought from Asia, were
used as watch-dogs even in Roman times.
Now that a tunnel has been built through
the mountains, the Pass is less dangerous,
but each year, the dogs are still sent out
15 into the snow whenever a traveller is in
difficulty. Despite the new tunnel, there

These friendly dogs . . .

are still a few people who rashly attempt to cross the Pass on foot.
    During the summer months, the monastery is very busy, for it is visited by
thousands of people who cross the Pass in cars. As there are so many people
20 about, the dogs have to be kept in a special enclosure. In winter, however, life
at the monastery is quite different. The temperature drops to −30° and very
few people attempt to cross the Pass. The monks prefer winter to summer for
they have more privacy. The dogs have greater freedom, too, for they are
allowed to wander outside their enclosure. The only regular visitors to the
25 monastery in winter are parties of skiers who go there at Christmas and Easter.
These young people, who love the peace of the mountains, always receive a warm
welcome at St Bernard's monastery.

Comprehension and Précis

In not more than 80 words give an account of life at St Bernard's Monastery in summer
and in winter. Do not include anything that is not in the last paragraph.
Answer these questions in note form to get your points:
  1. When is St Bernard's monastery visited by thousands of people?
  2. How do these people cross the Pass?
  3. Why are the dogs kept in a special enclosure?
  4. How low does the temperature drop in winter?
  5. Are there few visitors then, or are there a great many?
  6. Do the monks prefer the winter season or not?
  7. What are the dogs free to do in winter?
  8. What sort of people regularly visit the monastery in winter?
  9. Do they stay there the whole winter, or do they stay only at certain times?
  10. Are they warmly welcomed or not?

Vocabulary

Give another word or phrase to replace the following words as they are used in the
passage: famous (l. 4); founded (l. 5); lies (l. 6); now that (l. 12); rashly attempt (l.17);
quite (l. 21); drops (l. 21).

Composition

In not more than 200 words, write an imaginary account of the way a traveller was rescued on St Bernard's Pass in winter. Use the ideas given below. Do not write more than three paragraphs.

Title: Rescue.

Introduction: A monk took two dogs out for exercise—the dogs were restless—a search party was organized.

Development: The dogs led the monks through the snow—high winds the previous night—now heavy fog—temperature 20° below—they got near—heard cries—a man was trapped under the snow—the dogs dragged him out—he was taken to the monastery on a sledge.

Conclusion: The man was unconscious—recovered later—told them what had happened the previous night.

Letter-writing

Write a letter of about 80 words to a friend recommending a hotel in the Alps to him. Supply a suitable Introduction and Conclusion. Use the following ideas to write the *Purpose:* why you recommend it—you stayed there last year—fine views—healthy mountain air—comfortable—moderate prices—you intend to go this year as well.

Key Structures

Verb-forms: review. (1 KS 206)

Exercises

A. Underline the verbs in the passage which tell us *what always happens, what happened* and *what has happened.* Note how they have been used.

B. Write sentences using the following words and phrases: ago; for six months; when; since 1948.

Special Difficulties

The dogs are still sent out into the snow whenever a traveller is in difficulty. (ll. 14–16) Compare these pairs of sentences:

He did what I asked him to do.
He did whatever I asked him to do.

Who told you that?
Whoever told you that?

I'll tell you when you make a mistake.
I'll tell you whenever you make a mistake.

Where has he gone?
Wherever has he gone?

The word *-ever* is sometimes used in this way to give emphasis to words like who, which, and what.

Exercise

Supply the missing words in the following sentences:
1. Now that he's grown up, he does . . .-ever he pleases.
2. . . .-ever I telephone, the line's engaged.
3. . . .-ever told you that, didn't know what he was talking about.

9 A Trip to Mars

By now, a rocket will have set off on its
35 million mile trip to Mars and scientists must be waiting anxiously for the
results. The rocket will be travelling for
5   six months before it reaches the planet.
It contains a number of scientific instruments, including a television camera. Any
pictures that are taken will have to travel
for three minutes before they reach the
10   earth. If the pictures are successful, they
may solve a number of problems about
Mars and provide information about the
markings on its surface which, nearly 100
years ago, the astronomer, Schiaparelli,
15   thought to be canals.

A rubber ball could be dropped

It will be a long time before any
landing on Mars can be attempted. This will only be possible when scientists
have learnt a lot more about the atmosphere that surrounds the planet. If a
satellite can one day be put into orbit round Mars, scientists will be able to find
20   out a great deal. An interesting suggestion for measuring the atmosphere around
Mars has been put forward. A rubber ball containing a radio transmitter could
be dropped from a satellite so that it would fall towards the surface of the planet.
The radio would signal the rate at which the ball was slowed down and scientists
would be able to calculate how dense the atmosphere is. It may even be possible
25   to drop a capsule containing scientific instruments on to the planet's surface.
Only when a great deal more information has been obtained, will it be possible
to plan a manned trip to Mars.

Comprehension and Précis

In not more than 80 words describe how it will be possible for scientists to learn a
great deal about Mars and about the atmosphere which surrounds it. Do not include
anything that is not in the last paragraph.

Answer these questions in note form to get your points:

1. What must scientists learn about Mars before anyone attempts to go there?
2. What could be dropped from a satellite?
3. What would the ball contain?
4. How would scientists be able to calculate the density of the atmosphere?
5. In what other way could information about Mars be obtained?

Vocabulary

Give another word or phrase to replace the following words as they are used in the
passage: travelling (l. 4); reaches (l. 5); contains (l. 6); solve (l. 11); provide (l. 12);
markings (l. 13); surface (l. 13); thought (l. 15).

Composition

Describe an imaginary trip to the moon. Expand the following into a paragraph of
about 150 words.

Once the rocket had got beyond the earth's atmosphere, the moon looked like a . . . The astronauts, who had been specially trained for this difficult journey . . . After the rocket landed on the moon, the astronauts got out and . . . They were wearing heavy suits so that . . . The astronauts explored a . . . They collected . . . from the surface of the moon. The moon landscape was . . . It would be impossible for human beings to live there because . . . From this distance, the earth looked like . . . After the astronauts had . . . the rocket began its long journey back to earth.   (91 words)

Letter-writing

You borrowed a book from a friend but your baby tore some of the pages. Write a letter of about 80 words offering to replace it. Supply a suitable Introduction and Conclusion. Use the following ideas to write the *Purpose*: very sorry for what has happened—had left book on low table—baby got hold of it—tore several pages—you have bought another book and are sending it.

Key Structures

What will happen? Review: **1 KS 208, 210.**

Exercises
A. Study the use in the passage of all the verbs which express the future.

B. Give the correct form of the verbs in brackets. Do not refer to the passage until you finish the exercise:
By now, a rocket (set off) on its 35 million mile trip to Mars. The rocket (travel) for six months before it (reach) the planet. Any pictures that are taken (have to) travel for three minutes before they (reach) the earth.

Special Difficulties

Scientists must be waiting anxiously for the results. (ll. 2–4)
Read these sentences:
I shall be waiting for you at the station. (**1 KS 37**)
By this time tomorrow, the *Astra* will have been flying through space for seventeen hours. (**1 KS 151**)
We can use the verbs can, could, may, might and must in the same way. Study these examples:
Why are you wasting time? You could be finishing your work.
My aunt may be coming here tomorrow.
Tom isn't here. He must be working in the garden.
We could have been flying to Spain now if we had bought tickets in time.
You may have been trying harder, but your work is still not good enough.
I'm sorry I'm late. You must have been waiting a long time.

Exercise
Supply the correct form of the verbs in brackets:
1. Jimmy's upstairs. He (must/do) his homework.
2. Jimmy was upstairs. He (must/do) his homework.
3. I wish it wasn't raining. We (could/play) tennis.
4. We (must/wait) for the bus for over an hour before it arrived.

10 The Loss of the 'Titanic'

The great ship, *Titanic*, sailed for New
York from Southampton on April 10th,
1912. She was carrying 1316 passengers
and a crew of 891. Even by modern
standards, the 46,000 ton *Titanic* was a
colossal ship. At that time, however, she
was not only the largest ship that had
ever been built, but was regarded as
unsinkable, for she had sixteen water-
tight compartments. Even if two of these
were flooded, she would still be able to
float. The tragic sinking of this great
liner will always be remembered, for she
went down on her first voyage with heavy
loss of life.

*the icy waters of the
North Atlantic*

Four days after setting out, while the
Titanic was sailing across the icy waters of the North Atlantic, a huge iceberg
was suddenly spotted by a look-out. After the alarm had been given, the great
ship turned sharply to avoid a direct collision. The *Titanic* turned just in time,
narrowly missing the immense wall of ice which rose over 100 feet out of the
water beside her. Suddenly, there was a slight trembling sound from below, and
the captain went down to see what had happened. The noise had been so faint
that no one thought that the ship had been damaged. Below, the captain realized
to his horror that the *Titanic* was sinking rapidly, for five of her sixteen water-
tight compartments had already been flooded! The order to abandon ship was
given and hundreds of people plunged into the icy water. As there were not
enough life-boats for everybody, 1500 lives were lost.

Comprehension and Précis

Write an account of the sinking of the *Titanic in not more than 80 words*. Do not include
anything that is not in the last paragraph.
Answer these questions in note form to get your points:
1. Where was the *Titanic* sailing?
2. What was seen by a look-out?
3. When did the ship turn sharply?
4. Did it sail alongside the iceberg, or did it collide with it?
5. What was heard from below?
6. What did the captain do?
7. What did he find?
8. When did everyone jump overboard?
9. Why were 1500 people drowned?

Vocabulary

Give another word or phrase to replace the following words as they are used in the
passage: colossal (l. 6); regarded (l. 8); compartments (l. 10); flooded (l. 11); float (l. 12);
avoid (l. 19); narrowly (l. 20).

Composition

In not more than 200 words write an imaginary account of what happened on the *Titanic* immediately after the order to abandon ship was given. Use the ideas given below. Do not write more than three paragraphs.

Title : Abandon Ship.

Introduction : Order to abandon ship unexpected—everybody unprepared.

Development : Immediate effect—panic and confusion—people rushing in all directions —crew came up from below—life-boats lowered—people jumped overboard—struggle to get into life-boats—life-boats full.

Conclusion.: *Titanic* sank rapidly—people in water—cries of despair—life-boats moved away.

Letter-writing

Which of the following addresses is correct:

19 Kingsley Ave.	19 Kingsley Ave.,	19 Kingsley Ave.,
Sandford Park,	Sandford Park,	Sandford Park,
London, N.W.8,	London, N.W.8,	London, N.W.8,
England.	England.	England
August 24th, 19—	24th Aug., 19—	Aug. 24th, 19—

Key Structures

What had happened? (1 KS 212)

Exercises

A. Underline the verbs in the passage which tell us *what had happened*. Note how they have been used.

B. Give the correct form of the verbs in brackets. Do not refer to the passage until you finish the exercise.

1. At that time, she was the largest ship that ever (build).
2. After the alarm (give), the great ship (turn) sharply to avoid a direct collision.

Special Difficulties

Word Building.

Study these sentences:

He works hard. He is a hard worker.

He plays the violin. He is a violinist.

He is very careless. I have never seen such carelessness.

Can you explain this? Can you give me an explanation?

He has a responsible position. He has a lot of responsibility.

Note how new words can be formed by adding *-er, -ist, -ness, -ion, -ity.*

Exercise

Supply the missing words in the following sentences:

1. He studied physics at university. He is a p . . .
2. He works in a mine. He is a m . . .
3. Pasteur did a great service to . . . (human).
4. He is trying to make a good . . . (impress).
5. His paintings have been admired for their . . . (original).

11 Not Guilty

[handwritten: Direct Speech.]

Going through the Customs is a tiresome business. The strangest thing about it is that really honest people are often made to feel guilty. The hardened professional
5 smuggler, on the other hand, is never troubled by such feelings, even if he has five hundred gold watches hidden in his suitcase. When I returned from abroad recently, a particularly officious young
10 Customs Officer clearly regarded me as a smuggler.

often made to feel guilty

'Have you anything to declare?' he asked, looking me in the eye.
'No,' I answered confidently.
15 'Would you mind unlocking this suit-case please?'
'Not at all,' I answered.
The Officer went through the case with great care. All the things I had packed so carefully were soon in a dreadful mess. I felt sure I would never be able to
20 close the case again. Suddenly, I saw the Officer's face light up. He had spotted a tiny bottle at the bottom of my case and he pounced on it with delight.
'Perfume, eh?' he asked sarcastically. 'You should have declared that. Perfume is not exempt from import duty.'
'But it isn't perfume,' I said. 'It's hair-oil.' Then I added with a smile, 'It's
25 a strange mixture I make myself.'
As I expected, he did not believe me.
'Try it!' I said encouragingly.
The Officer unscrewed the cap and put the bottle to his nostrils. He was greeted by an unpleasant smell which convinced him that I was telling the truth.
30 A few minutes later, I was able to hurry away with precious chalk-marks on my baggage.

Comprehension and Précis

In not more than 80 words describe the experiences of the writer while he was going through the Customs. Do not include anything that is not in the passage.
Answer these questions in note form to get your points:

1. Did the writer have anything to declare or not?
2. What did the Customs Officer make him do?
3. Did the Customs Officer search the case carefully or not?
4. What did he find?
5. What did he think was in the bottle?
6. What did the writer tell him the bottle contained?
7. Who had made it?
8. Did the Customs Officer believe him or not?
9. What did the writer encourage the Officer to do?
10. What convinced the Officer that the writer was telling the truth?
11. Did the Officer let the writer pass through the Customs or not?

Vocabulary

Give another word or phrase to replace the following words as they are used in the passage: troubled (l. 6); clearly (l. 10); packed (l. 18); dreadful (l. 19); cap (l. 28); nostrils (l. 28); convinced (l. 29).

Composition

Imagine that a man tries to smuggle something valuable through the Customs. Expand the following into a paragraph of about 150 words.

When the Customs Officer . . . the man said that he had nothing to declare. The Officer asked the man to . . . Although the case contained only . . . and . . . it was very heavy. This made the Officer suspicious, so he . . . The case was soon empty and when the Officer . . . he found that . . . The Officer examined the case carefully and saw that . . . He . . . and removed the bottom part of the case which contained . . . While the Officer was looking at . . . the man tried to . . . For a moment, the man disappeared among . . . but he was soon . . . and placed under arrest.   (93 words)

Letter-writing

A friend has written to you asking you to lend him some money. Write a letter of about 80 words telling him you cannot afford to. Supply a suitable Introduction and Conclusion. Use the following ideas to write the *Purpose*: sorry you cannot help—have a great many expenses—you are in debt yourself—suggest someone who might help.

Key Structures

He said that . . . He told me . . . He asked me . . . (1 KS 214)

Exercise
Answer these questions:
Lines 22–23 What did the Customs Officer tell the writer he should have done? Why did he tell the writer this?
Lines 24–25 What did the writer tell the Customs Officer?
Line 27 What did he tell the Customs Officer to do?

Special Difficulties

Capital Letters.
Note how capital letters have been used in these sentences:
The train came into the station. It arrived at 5 o'clock.
George lives in Canada. He is Canadian. He is not an American.
I'll see you on Tuesday, January 14th.
Have you read 'Great Expectations'?

Exercise
Write this paragraph again using full stops and capital letters where necessary:
because tim jones cannot speak french or german he never enjoys travelling abroad last march, however, he went to denmark and stayed in copenhagen he said he spent most of his time at the tivoli which is one of the biggest funfairs in the world at the tivoli you can enjoy yourself very much even if you don't speak danish.

12   Life on a Desert Island

Most of us have formed an unrealistic
picture of life on a desert island. We
sometimes imagine a desert island to be a
sort of paradise where the sun always
5 shines. Life there is simple and good.
Ripe fruit falls from the trees and you
never have to work. The other side of the
picture is quite the opposite. Life on a
desert island is wretched. You either
10 starve to death or live like Robinson
Crusoe, waiting for a boat which never
comes. Perhaps there is an element of
truth in both these pictures, but few of us
have had the opportunity to find out.

'ate like kings'

15   Two men who recently spent five days
on a coral island wished they had stayed
there longer. They were taking a badly damaged boat from the Virgin Islands to
Miami to have it repaired. During the journey, their boat began to sink. They
quickly loaded a small rubber dinghy with food, matches, and tins of beer and
20 rowed for a few miles across the Caribbean until they arrived at a tiny coral
island. There were hardly any trees on the island and there was no water, but
this did not prove to be a problem. The men collected rain-water in the rubber
dinghy. As they had brought a spear gun with them, they had plenty to eat.
They caught lobster and fish every day, and, as one of them put it 'ate like
25 kings'. When a passing tanker rescued them five days later, both men were
genuinely sorry that they had to leave.

Comprehension and Précis

In not more than 80 words explain how the two men came to spend five days on a
desert island and say what they did there. Do not include anything that is not in the
last paragraph.
Answer these questions to get your points:
1. Was the men's boat damaged or not?
2. Where were they taking it?
3. What happened to it on the way?
4. What did the men load on to their rubber dinghy?
5. Where did they row?
6. Where did they arrive?
7. Where did the men collect water during their stay there?
8. How did they catch fish and lobster?
9. Did they eat 'like Kings' for five days or not?
10. How were they rescued?

Vocabulary

Give another word or phrase to replace the following words as they are used in the
passage: picture (l. 2); wretched (l. 9); starve to death (l. 10); opportunity (l. 14);
repaired (l. 18); loaded (l. 19); dinghy (l. 19).

Composition

(handwritten) ① Arrival, ② Survival, ③ Departure

Imagine spending two weeks on an uninhabited desert island. In not more than 200 words, describe what you did there. Use the ideas given below. Do not write more than three paragraphs.

Title: Shipwrecked.

Introduction: Shipwreck—everybody drowned—I clung to a plank—washed up on island.

Development: Slept for a long time—woke up—hungry and thirsty—explored island—uninhabited—found plenty of fruit—fresh-water spring—tried to hunt wild animals—failed to catch anything—spent days swimming, lying in sun.

Conclusion: Boat on horizon—signalled and shouted—rescued.

Letter-writing

In not more than 60 words, write a suitable *Purpose* and *Conclusion* to follow this introductory paragraph:

Dear Judy,

We arrived here late last night and are staying at a charming little hotel by the sea. The weather is perfect and I am sure we are going to enjoy our holiday.

Key Structures

If. (1 KS 216)

Exercise

Complete the following:

1. If you had told me earlier . . .
2. If I were you . . .
3. You will be disappointed if . . .
4. You would change your mind if . . .

Special Difficulties

They wished they had stayed there longer. (ll. 16–17)

Wish and If only. Study these examples:

I wish you would do as you are told. *(handwritten: not hopeful state)*

If only the weather would change.

I wish she could see me now.

I wish I had more time to spare.

If only you would try a little harder!

I wish I hadn't said anything about it.

If only we could have gone to the party!

I wish you hadn't spent so much money.

Exercise

Complete the following:

1. It was silly of me not to buy that dress. I wish I . . .
2. You are making a lot of noise. I wish you . . .
3. It's a pity John's away. If only he . . .
4. He plays the piano so well. I wish I . . .
5. I never studied at all when I was at school. I wish I . . .
6. I'm sorry I mentioned it to him. I wish I . . .

13 'It's Only Me'

After her husband had gone to work, Mrs Richards sent her children to school and went upstairs to her bedroom. She was too excited to do any housework that
5 morning, for in the evening she would be going to a fancy dress party with her husband. She intended to dress up as a ghost and as she had made her costume the night before, she was impatient to try
10 it on. Though the costume consisted only of a sheet, it was very effective. After putting it on, Mrs Richards went downstairs. She wanted to find out whether it would be comfortable to wear.

*She tried to explain
the situation*

15 Just as Mrs Richards was entering the dining-room, there was a knock on the front door. She knew that it must be the baker. She had told him to come straight in if ever she failed to open the door and to leave the bread on the kitchen table. Not wanting to frighten the poor man, Mrs Richards quickly hid
20 in the small store-room under the stairs. She heard the front door open and heavy footsteps in the hall. Suddenly the door of the store-room was opened and a man entered. Mrs Richards realized that it must be the man from the Electricity Board who had come to read the meter. She tried to explain the situation, saying 'It's only me', but it was too late. The man let out a cry and
25 jumped back several paces. When Mrs Richards walked towards him, he fled, slamming the door behind him.

Comprehension and Précis

In not more than 80 words describe what happened from the moment Mrs Richards entered the dining-room. Do not include anything that is not in the last paragraph. Answer these questions in note form to get your points:
   1. How was Mrs Richards dressed?
   2. Where was she going when someone knocked at the door?
   3. Whom did she think it was?
   4. Where did she hide?
   5. Did she hear footsteps in the hall or not?
   6. Who suddenly opened the store-room door?
   7. What did she say to him?
   8. Did he get a bad fright or not?
   9. Did she walk towards him or not?
   10. Did he flee or did he stay there?
   11. Did he slam the front door or not?

Vocabulary

Give another word or phrase to replace the following words as they are used in the passage: intended (l. 7); impatient (l. 9); try it on (ll. 9–10); whether (l. 13); failed to (l. 18); fled (l. 25); slamming (l. 26).

Composition

Imagine that the man from the Electricity Board returned to Mrs Richards' house with a policeman. Mrs Richards was no longer dressed as a ghost. Expand the following into a paragraph of about 150 words.

Mrs Richards immediately went upstairs and . . . She felt sorry for the poor man from . . . but at the same time, she was . . . Suddenly, there was a knock at the front door and Mrs Richards . . . The electricity man had returned, accompanied . . . so she . . . The man told Mrs Richards that . . . and that . . . Though Mrs Richards explained that . . . he refused to believe her. She told him to open the store-room door but he . . . so she . . . While the electricity man and the policeman . . . , Mrs Richards fetched . . . She showed it . . . and . . .   (85 words)

Letter-writing

Put yourself in the position of the electricity man. Imagine you are writing a letter of about 80 words to your mother describing your experience. Supply a suitable Introduction and Conclusion. Use the following ideas to write the *Purpose*: you got a terrible shock—house haunted—ghost under stairs—it ran after you—you fled—the story is really true.

Key Structures

Must. (1 **KS 218**)
Exercises
A. Note how *must* has been used in lines 17 and 22.

B. Write three pairs of sentences using the following:
1. *must go* and *must be*.   2. *mustn't* and *needn't*.   3. *had to* and *ought to have*.

Special Difficulties

It would be comfortable to wear. (ll. 13–14)
Instead of saying: I was sorry *when I learnt* that he had had an accident.
We can say: I was sorry *to learn* that he had had an accident.
Study these examples:
He was *delighted to learn* that his offer had been accepted.
I was *glad to hear* that he had arrived.
I was *pleased to hear* that you now feel better.
He was *anxious to leave* early.

Exercises
A. Write these sentences again changing the form of the words in italics:
1. I was glad *when I heard* that she had gone away for ever.
2. He said he was sorry *if he had* upset me.
3. You will be sad *when you hear* what I have to tell you.

B. Write sentences using the following: pleased to; proud to; delighted to; shocked to.

14　A Noble Gangster

There was a time when the owners of shops and businesses in Chicago had to pay large sums of money to gangsters in return for 'protection'. If the money was
5　not paid promptly, the gangsters would quickly put a man out of business by destroying his shop. Obtaining 'protection money' is not a modern crime. As long ago as the fourteenth century, an
10　Englishman, Sir John Hawkwood, made the remarkable discovery that people would rather pay large sums of money than have their life work destroyed by gangsters.

. . . made the remarkable discovery

15　　Six hundred years ago, Sir John Hawkwood arrived in Italy with a band of soldiers and settled near Florence. He soon made a name for himself and came to be known to the Italians as Giovanni Acuto. Whenever the Italian city-states were at war with each other, Hawkwood used to hire his soldiers to princes who
20　were willing to pay the high price he demanded. In times of peace, when business was bad, Hawkwood and his men would march into a city-state and, after burning down a few farms, would offer to go away if protection money was paid to them. Hawkwood made large sums of money in this way. In spite of this, the Italians regarded him as a sort of hero. When he died at the age of
25　eighty, the Florentines gave him a state funeral and had a picture painted which was dedicated to the memory of 'the most valiant soldier and most notable leader, Signor Giovanni Haukodue'.

Comprehension and Précis

In not more than 80 words write an account of Sir John Hawkwood's career from the time he arrived in Italy. Do not include anything that is not in the last paragraph. Answer these questions in note form to get your points:
1. Where did Sir John Hawkwood settle six hundred years ago?
2. Whom did he hire soldiers to in times of war?
3. Would he threaten to destroy a city-state in times of peace or not?
4. When would he spare a city-state?
5. Did the Italians regard him as a hero in spite of this or not?
6. How old was he when he died?
7. Who gave him a state funeral when he died?
8. Did they have a picture painted or not?
9. What was it dedicated to?

Vocabulary

Give another word or phrase to replace the following words as they are used in the passage: sums (l. 3); promptly (l. 5); obtaining (l. 7); remarkable (l. 11); settled (l. 17); hire (l. 19); demanded (l. 20).

Composition

In not more than 200 words write an imaginary account of one of Sir John Hawkwood's exploits. Use the ideas given below. Do not write more than three paragraphs.

Title: Hawkwood Defeated.

Introduction: News that Hawkwood and his men were approaching—panic—villagers prepared to defend farms.

Development: Farmers fought—poorly armed—many killed—Hawkwood destroyed farms—sent message to prince of city-state—demanded money—refused—battle followed—Hawkwood invaded city—many buildings were destroyed—people killed.

Conclusion: Hawkwood was driven off—never attacked this city again—later became the prince's friend.

Letter-writing

You had agreed to give a talk at your local library, but now find that you are unable to do so. Write a letter of about 80 words explaining why. Supply a suitable Introduction and Conclusion. Use the following ideas to write the *Purpose:* sorry for the inconvenience—you are being sent abroad by your firm—will be away for three weeks—hope to give a talk on a later occasion.

Key Structures

Have. (1 **KS 220**)

Exercises

A. Note how *have* has been used in lines 13 and 25.

B. Write sentences using *have* with the following:
1. a smoke.   2. got a headache.   3. repaired.

Special Difficulties

People would rather pay large sums of money than ... (ll. 11–13)

Instead of saying:	*We can say:*
I prefer to wait here.	I would rather wait here.
	Or: I would sooner wait here.
I prefer not to wait here.	I would rather not wait here.
	Or: I would sooner not wait here.
It would be better if he waited here.	I'd rather *he waited* here.
It would be better if he didn't wait here.	I'd rather *he didn't wait* here.

Exercise

Give the correct form of the verbs in brackets:
1. I'd rather (go) to the cinema.
2. I'd rather he (leave) earlier.
3. I'd rather you not (speak) to him.
4. I'd rather not (speak) about it.
5. I'd rather my father (settle) the account.
6. She'd rather you not (tell) anyone about it.

15 Sixpence Worth of Trouble

a source.
a way
— a main

grateful
feel happy

Children always appreciate small gifts of
money. Father, of course, provides a
regular supply of pocket-money, but
uncles and aunts are always a source of
5 extra income. With some children, small
sums go a long way. If sixpences are not
exchanged for sweets, they rattle for
months inside money-boxes. Only very
thrifty children manage to fill up a
10 money-box. For most of them, sixpence
is a small price to pay for a satisfying bar
of chocolate.

The fire-brigade was called

My nephew, George, has a money-box
but it is always empty. Very few of the
15 sixpences I have given him have found
their way there. I gave him sixpence
yesterday and advised him to save it. Instead, he bought himself sixpence
worth of trouble. On his way to the sweet shop, he dropped his sixpence and it
rolled along the pavement and then disappeared down a drain. George took off
20 his jacket, rolled up his sleeves and pushed his right arm through the drain
cover. He could not find his sixpence anywhere, and what is more, he could not
get his arm out. A crowd of people gathered round him and a lady rubbed his
apartment
arm with soap and butter, but George was firmly stuck. The fire-brigade was
called and two firemen freed George using a special type of grease. George was
25 not too upset by his experience because the lady who owns the sweet shop
heard about his troubles and rewarded him with a large box of chocolates.

Comprehension and Précis   *Stick – stuck*

Strike
Struck

In not more than 80 words describe George's experiences after his uncle gave him
sixpence. Do not include anything that is not in the last paragraph.
Answer these questions in note form to get your points:

1. Where was George going?
2. Where did he lose his sixpence?
3. Did he take his jacket off or not?
4. Where did he put his arm?
5. Did he find his sixpence, or did he fail to find it?
6. Could he get his arm out or not?
7. Did a crowd of people gather round him or not?
8. What did a lady try to do?
9. Did she succeed or did she fail?
10. How did firemen finally free George?
11. What did the owner of the sweet shop present him with?

Vocabulary

Give another word or phrase to replace the following words as they are used in the
passage: appreciate (l. 1); gifts (l. 1); extra income (l. 5); rattle (l. 7); price (l. 11);
gathered (l. 22); was firmly stuck (l. 23).

buy — bought
bring — brought

Composition

Suppose you were among the crowd of people that gathered round George. Write an imaginary account of what happened. Expand the following into a paragraph of about 150 words.

I was walking along the street when I . . . I could hear people shouting and . . . On arriving at the scene, I . . . A lady carrying a large bar of soap and a saucepan full of water . . . She asked the boy if . . . Then she rubbed his arm with butter, but . . . Meanwhile, someone had telephoned . . . The boy had begun to cry, but when . . . At first, the firemen decided to . . . but they changed their minds and . . . The boy was soon free and though his arm hurt, he . . .   (82 words)

Letter-writing

Write a letter of about 80 words to your eight-year-old nephew asking him what he would like you to buy him for his birthday. Supply a suitable Introduction and Conclusion. Use the following information to write the *Purpose*: you want to get him something he will really like—a few suggestions—ask him to let you know what he wants—you will send it by post so that it arrives on his birthday.

Key Structures

Can. (1 KS 222)

Exercises
A. Note how the following have been used in the passage:
manage to (l. 9) and could not (l. 21).

B. Write sentences using each of the following:
1. was able to.   2. could.   3. managed to.

Special Difficulties

Only very thrifty children manage to fill up a money-box. (ll. 8–10)
Note the use of *up* in these sentences:
We drove up to the farmhouse.
The children ran up the garden path to greet their father.
I didn't like my composition so I tore it up.
He has built up a large collection of stamps.

Exercise
Complete these sentences using the correct form of the following verbs: do, save, wind, sail, wrap, button, go, eat.
1. If I can . . . up enough money, I shall go abroad.
2. The steam-boat . . . up the river.
3. It was very cold so I . . . up my coat before going out.
4. . . . up what is on your plate and I'll give you some more.
5. I . . . up to a policeman and asked him the way to the station.
6. He . . . the fish up in a piece of newspaper.
7. My watch has stopped because I forgot to . . . it up.
8. It takes children a long time to learn how to . . . up their shoe-laces.

16 Mary had a Little Lamb

Mary and her husband Dimitri lived in
the tiny village of Perachora in southern
Greece. One of Mary's prize possessions
was a little white lamb which her husband
5 had given her. She kept it tied to a tree
in a field during the day and went to
fetch it every evening. One evening, however, the lamb was missing. The rope had
been cut, so it was obvious that the lamb
10 had been stolen.

*the little black lamb was
almost white*

When Dimitri came in from the fields,
his wife told him what had happened.
Dimitri at once set out to find the thief.
He knew it would not prove difficult in
15 such a small village. After telling several
of his friends about the theft, Dimitri
found out that his neighbour, Aleko, had suddenly acquired a new lamb.
Dimitri immediately went to Aleko's house and angrily accused him of stealing
the lamb. He told him he had better return it or he would call the police. Aleko
20 denied taking it and led Dimitri into his back-yard. It was true that he had just
bought a lamb, he explained, but *his* lamb was black. Ashamed of having acted
so rashly, Dimitri apologized to Aleko for having accused him. While they were
talking it began to rain and Dimitri stayed in Aleko's house until the rain stopped.
When he went outside half an hour later, he was astonished to find that the little
25 black lamb was almost white. Its wool, which had been dyed black, had been
washed clean by the rain!

Comprehension and Précis

In not more than 80 words describe what happened from the time when Dimitri learnt
that his wife's white lamb had been stolen. Do not include anything that is not in the
last paragraph.
Answer these questions in note form to get your points:
  1. What did Mary tell Dimitri when he came home?]
  2. What did Dimitri learn about his neighbour, Aleko?]
  3. Where did Dimitri go?]
  4. What did he accuse Aleko of?]
  5. Did Aleko show Dimitri his new lamb or not?]
  6. What colour was it?]
  7. What did Dimitri do when he saw it was black?]
  8. Why did Dimitri stay in Aleko's house for half an hour?]
  9. Why did he get a surprise when he went outside?]
  10. Had the lamb been dyed or not?]

Vocabulary

Give another word or phrase to replace the following words as they are used in the
passage: tiny (l. 2); fetch (l. 7); missing (l. 8); acquired (l. 17); denied (l. 20); apologized (l. 22); dyed (l. 25).

Composition

In not more than 200 words continue the above passage. Use the ideas given below. Do not write more than three paragraphs.

Title: Not So Black.

Introduction: Dimitri took a close look at the lamb—surprised—it was white—recognized it as his own.

Development: Angry scene—accusation—Aleko still denied theft—violent argument—finally Aleko admitted it—Dimitri called the police—Aleko was arrested—Dimitri took the lamb home.

Conclusion: Excitement in the village—villagers were amused by the event—discussed it at great length for a long time.

Letter-writing

The following events have prompted you to write letters. Write suitable introductions of about 25 words each.

1. A prize you have won.
2. An examination you have passed.

Key Structures

He accused him of stealing the lamb. (1 KS 224)

Exercises

A. Note the form of the verbs in italics: accused him of *stealing* (l. 18); Aleko denied *taking* it (ll. 19–20); ashamed of *having* acted . . . (l. 21); apologized for *having* accused (l. 22); it began *to rain* (l. 23).

B. Write sentences using the following:
1. We continued . . . 2. Let's go . . . 3. This shirt needs . . . 4. Excuse my . . .

Special Difficulties

He had better return it. (l. 19)

Instead of saying:	*We can say:*
It would be advisable for you to leave now.	You had better leave now.
It would not be advisable for you to telephone him.	You had better not telephone him.

Exercise

Rewrite the following sentences using *had better* in place of *it would be advisable*.
1. It would be advisable for us to have lunch.
2. It would be advisable for her to renew her passport.
3. It would not be advisable for you to ask so many questions.
4. It would not be advisable for us to stay any longer.
5. It would be advisable for the children to get an early night.
6. It would be advisable for me to consult my solicitor.

17   The Greatest Bridge in the World

Verrazano, an Italian about whom little is known, sailed into New York Harbour in 1524 and named it Angoulême. He described it as 'a very agreeable situation
5 located within two small hills in the midst of which flowed a great river.' Though Verrazano is by no means considered to be a great explorer, his name will probably remain immortal, for on November
10 21st, 1964, the greatest bridge in the world was named after him.

The Verrazano Bridge, which was designed by Othmar Ammann, joins Brooklyn to Staten Island. It has a span
15 of 4260 feet. The bridge is so long that the shape of the earth had to be taken

Sailed into New York harbour in 1524

into account by its designer. Two great towers support four huge cables. The towers are built on immense underwater platforms made of steel and concrete. The platforms extend to a depth of over 100 feet under the sea. These alone took
20 sixteen months to build. Above the surface of the water, the towers rise to a height of nearly 700 feet. They support the cables from which the bridge has been suspended. Each of the four cables contains 26,108 lengths of wire. It has been estimated that if the bridge were packed with cars, it would still only be carrying a third of its total capacity. However, size and strength are not the only
25 important things about this bridge. Despite its immensity, it is both simple and elegant, fulfilling its designer's dream to create 'an enormous object drawn as faintly as possible'.

Comprehension and Précis

Describe the Verrazano Bridge *in not more than 80 words*. Do not include anything that is not in the last paragraph.
Answer these questions in note form to get your points:
1. What is the name of the bridge which joins Brooklyn to Staten Island?
2. What is its span?
3. How many towers has it got?
4. What do these towers support?
5. What are the towers built on?
6. How far under the sea do the platforms go?
7. How far above the surface do the towers rise?
8. What is the bridge suspended from?
9. How many lengths of wire does each of these cables contain?
10. Is the bridge very strong or not?
11. Is it simple and elegant or not?

Vocabulary

Give another word or phrase to replace the following words as they are used in the passage: agreeable situation (l. 4); midst (l. 5); considered (l. 7); remain immortal (l. 9); span (l. 14); taken into account (ll. 16–17); support (l. 17).

Composition

Describe any bridge you know well. Expand the following into a paragraph of about 150 words.

The bridge I know best is called . . . It joins . . . to . . . From far away it looks . . . but when you get near . . . It is made of . . . and supported by . . . which . . . If you stand on the bridge early in the morning, you can see . . . At this time everything is quiet. During the day, however, . . . I enjoy standing on the bridge at night when . . . In the darkness, you can see . . . In the stillness . . . are the only sounds that can be heard.   (77 words)

Letter-writing

A friend who is coming to visit you has written to you asking for detailed information on how to get to your house. Write a reply in about 80 words. Supply a suitable Introduction and Conclusion. Use the following information to write the *Purpose*: which train to catch—where to get off—which bus to catch and where—any familiar landmark—where to get off—which road to take—where your house is.

Key Structures

The Verrazano bridge was designed by Othmar Ammann. (1 KS 226)

Exercise
Change the form of the verbs in these sentences. Omit the words in italics. Do not refer to the passage until you finish the exercise:
1. Verrazano is an Italian about whom *we* know little.
2. *They* do not consider Verrazano to be a great explorer.
3. *They* named the greatest bridge in the world after him.
4. *He* had to take into account the shape of the earth.
5. *They* have estimated that if the bridge were packed with cars . . .

Special Difficulties

He is by no means considered to be a great explorer. (ll. 7–8) Compare 1 SD 208.
Instead of saying: I find that he is quite unsuitable for the job.
We can say: I find him to be quite unsuitable for the job.

Exercise
Write these sentences again changing the form of the phrases in italics:
1. I believed *that he owned* property abroad.
2. The Minister declared *that the treaty was* invalid.
3. I know *that he is* a person of high integrity.
4. I guess *that he is* about twenty-seven years old.
5. We estimated *that this picture* is worth at least £500.

18 Electric Currents in Modern Art

Modern sculpture rarely surprises us any more. The idea that modern art can only be seen in museums is mistaken. Even people who take no interest in art cannot
5 have failed to notice examples of modern sculpture on display in public places. Strange forms stand in gardens, and outside buildings and shops. We have got quite used to them. Some so-called
10 'modern' pieces have been on display for nearly fifty years.

some people—including myself
—were surprised

In spite of this, some people—including myself—were surprised by a recent exhibition of modern sculpture.
15 The first thing I saw when I entered the art gallery was a notice which said: 'Do not touch the exhibits. Some of them are dangerous!' The objects on display were pieces of moving sculpture. Oddly shaped forms that are suspended from the ceiling and move in response to a gust of wind are quite familiar to every-
20 body. These objects, however, were different. Lined up against the wall, there were long thin wires attached to metal spheres. The spheres had been magnetized and attracted or repelled each other all the time. In the centre of the hall, there were a number of tall structures which contained coloured lights. These lights flickered continuously like traffic lights which have gone mad. Sparks
25 were emitted from small black boxes and red lamps flashed on and off angrily. It was rather like an exhibition of prehistoric electronic equipment. These peculiar forms not only seemed designed to shock people emotionally, but to give them electric shocks as well!

Comprehension and Précis

In not more than 80 words describe what the writer saw from the moment he entered the art gallery. Do not include anything that is not in the last paragraph.
Answer these questions in note form to get your points:
1. What did the writer see when he entered the art gallery?
2. Why did it forbid people to touch the exhibits?
3. What did the exhibition consist of?
4. What did the writer see against the wall?
5. What did the spheres do?
6. What did the tall structures in the centre of the hall contain?
7. What did the coloured lights do?
8. What was emitted from black boxes?
9. Did red lamps go on and off or not?

Vocabulary

Give another word or phrase to replace the following words as they are used in the passage: on display (l. 6); oddly (l. 18); suspended (l. 18); response (l. 19); familiar (l. 19); attached (l. 21); flickered continuously (l. 24).

Composition

In not more than 200 words describe an exhibition of modern paintings (real or imaginary). Use the ideas given below. Do not write more than three paragraphs.

Title: An Interesting Exhibition.

Introduction: Work of many artists exhibited—great public interest—you went to the art gallery.

Development: Description of some of the pictures on display—the picture you liked best—the strangest picture of them all.

Conclusion: People's comments overheard—your opinion of the paintings at the exhibition.

Letter-writing

Write a letter of about 80 words to a friend accepting an invitation to go with him to an exhibition. Supply a suitable Introduction and Conclusion. Use the following information to write the *Purpose*: thank him for invitation—looking forward to meeting him again soon—particularly interested in the exhibition—why—where you will meet your friend: time and place.

Key Structures

1 KS 228.

Exercise

Supply the missing words in the following sentences. Do not refer to the passage until you finish the exercise.

1. Even people who take no interest . . . art cannot have failed to notice examples of modern sculpture . . . display in public places.
2. We have got quite used . . . them.
3. Oddly shaped forms that are suspended . . . the ceiling and move . . . response . . . a gust of wind are quite familiar . . . everybody.
4. There were long thin wires attached . . . metal spheres.

Special Difficulties

Spelling.

Note the spelling of the words in italics:

I'll *pay* the bill. He never *pays* his bills.

He owns a *donkey*. I own two *donkeys*.

You'll wake up the *baby*. *Babies* often cry.

Will he *try* again? He never *tries* very hard.

Exercise

Add *s* or *ies* to the following words. Make any other necessary changes:

lady, supply, valley, qualify, story, day, say, reply, marry, way, chimney, hurry, stay, enjoy, buy, body, bury, fry.

19 A Very Dear Cat

Kidnappers are rarely interested in animals, but they recently took considerable interest in Mrs Eleanor Ramsay's cat. Mrs Eleanor Ramsay, a very wealthy
5 old lady, has shared a flat with her cat, Rastus, for a great many years. Rastus leads an orderly life. He usually takes a short walk in the evenings and is always home by seven o'clock. One evening,
10 however, he failed to arrive. Mrs Ramsay got very worried. She looked everywhere for him but could not find him.

Rastus was in safe hands

Three days after Rastus' disappearance, Mrs Ramsay received an anonymous *sender with no name*
15 letter. The writer stated that Rastus was in safe hands and would be returned immediately if Mrs Ramsay paid a ransom of £1000. Mrs Ramsay was instructed to place the money in a cardboard box and to leave it outside her door. At first, she decided to go to the police, but fearing that she would never see Rastus again
20 —the letter had made that quite clear—she changed her mind. She drew £1000 from her bank and followed the kidnapper's instructions. The next morning, the box had disappeared but Mrs Ramsay was sure that the kidnapper would keep his word. Sure enough, Rastus arrived punctually at seven o'clock that evening. He looked very well, though he was rather thirsty, for he drank half a bottle of
25 milk. The police were astounded *astonished* when Mrs Ramsay told them what she had done. She explained that Rastus was very dear to her. Considering the amount she paid, he was dear in more ways than one!

Comprehension and Précis

In not more than 80 words describe how Mrs Ramsay's cat, Rastus, was returned to her. Do not include anything that is not in the last paragraph.
Answer these questions in note form to get your points:
1. When did Mrs Ramsay receive an anonymous letter? ⌉
2. How much money did the kidnapper demand for the return of the cat?⌉
3. What would happen if she went to the police? ⌉
4. Where did she have to put the money? ⌉
5. Where did she have to put the box? ⌉
6. How much did she draw from the bank? ⌉
7. Did she act on the kidnapper's instructions or not? ⌉
8. Had the money disappeared the following morning or not? ⌉
9. When did Rastus return to Mrs Ramsay? ⌉

Vocabulary

Give another word or phrase to replace the following words as they are used in the passage: rarely (l. 1); considerable (ll. 2–3); wealthy (l. 4); worried (l. 11); stated (l. 15); changed her mind (l. 20); word (l. 23).

Composition

Describe how the kidnapper came to know that Mrs Ramsay was so fond of her cat and how he stole it. Expand the following into a paragraph of about 150 words.

In a bar one night, Mr X was talking to a workman who told him that . . . The workman added that Mrs Ramsay . . . Every day, Mr X stood outside . . . As the cat . . . that it had regular habits. He also found out as much as he could about Mrs Ramsay and learnt that . . . One evening, as the cat was leaving the block of flats . . . He took the cat to . . . During the next three days, he walked past Mrs Ramsay's flat on several occasions and noticed that . . . Now that he was sure . . . he wrote . . . in which he . . .

(98 words)

Letter-writing

Write a letter of about 80 words to a former schoolmaster telling him briefly what you have been doing since you left school. Supply a suitable Introduction and Conclusion. Use the following information to write your *Purpose*: further studies since leaving school—how you got your present job—whether you like it and why—what you hope to do in the future.

Key Structures

Review of verb-forms. (1 KS 230)

Exercise
Underline all the verbs in the passage and note how they have been used.

Special Difficulties

The Comma.
Note how commas are used in the following sentences:
1. After we had visited the market, we returned home.
2. Mr Griffiths, the Prime Minister, said that his party would win the next election.
3. I bought pens, pencils, paper and a bottle of ink.
4. It was raining heavily and I was sure no one would be at the race course. There were, however, hundreds of people there.
5. The small boat, which took eleven weeks to cross the Atlantic, arrived at Plymouth yesterday.

Exercise
Insert commas where necessary in the following paragraph:
Before going home I went to the grocer's. Bill Smith the man who always serves me was very busy. This however did not worry me. On the contrary it gave me the opportunity to look round for several things I wanted. By the time my turn came I had already filled a basket with packets of biscuits tins of fruit bars of soap and two large bags of flour.

20   Pioneer Pilots

In 1908 Lord Northcliffe offered a prize of £1000 to the first man who would fly across the English Channel. Over a year passed before the first attempt was made.
5 On July 19th, 1909, in the early morning, Hubert Latham took off from the French coast in his plane the 'Antoinette IV'. He had travelled only seven miles across the Channel when his engine failed and he
10 was forced to land on the sea. The 'Antoinette' floated on the water until Latham was picked up by a ship.

the first person to greet him . . .

Two days later, Louis Bleriot arrived near Calais with a plane called 'No. XI'.
15 Bleriot had been making planes since 1905 and this was his latest model. A week before, he had completed a successful overland flight during which he covered twenty-six miles. Latham, however, did not give up easily. He, too, arrived near Calais on the same day with a new 'Antoinette'. It looked as if
20 there would be an exciting race across the Channel. Both planes were going to take off on July 25th, but Latham failed to get up early enough. After making a short test flight at 4.15 a.m., Bleriot set off half an hour later. His great flight lasted thirty seven minutes. When he landed near Dover, the first person to greet him was a local policeman. Latham made another attempt a week later
25 and got within half a mile of Dover, but he was unlucky again. His engine failed and he landed on the sea for the second time.

Comprehension and Précis

In not more than 80 words describe the attempts made by Bleriot and Latham to fly across the Channel from the time when they both arrived at Calais. Do not include anything that is not in the last paragraph.
Answer these questions in note form to get your points:
1. On what date did Bleriot and Latham arrive at Calais?
2. Did it look as if there would be a race or not?
3. When would it take place?
4. Why did Latham not take part in the race?
5. Did Bleriot make a short test flight before setting out or not?
6. How long did it take him to fly across the Channel?
7. Who greeted him when he arrived at Dover?
8. How near to Dover did Latham fly the following week?
9. Why did he have to land on the sea for the second time?

Vocabulary

Give another word or phrase to replace the following words as they are used in the passage: forced to land (l. 10); picked up (l. 12); completed (l. 17); covered (l. 18); test (l. 22); set off (l. 22); failed (l. 26).

Composition

Imagine yourself in Bleriot's position. In not more than 200 words, write a first-person account of the flight across the Channel. Use the ideas given below. Do not write more than three paragraphs.

Title: My Flight Across the Channel.

Introduction: Early morning—no sign of Latham—test flight—all well.

Development: Started off—could no longer see ship following below—suddenly alone—worried about direction—sea and sky—high winds—engine very hot—it began to rain—rain cooled engine—land ahead.

Conclusion: Flew in a circle—looked for a place to land—on field—two minutes later: policeman: bonjour!

Letter-writing

Suppose that you are at this moment on board an aeroplane. Write a letter of about 80 words describing your impressions. Supply a suitable Introduction and Conclusion. Use the following ideas to write the *Purpose*: your feelings when the plane took off—how you feel now—height and speed—the view from the window—when you will arrive at your destination.

Special Difficulties

Review **SD 13-45**.

Exercises

A. Complete the following sentences:
1. What are you looking . . . (**SD 13**)
2. We have received fifty applications . . . all. (**SD 15**)
3. I happened to . . . (**SD 17**)
4. It happened . . . (**SD 17**)
5. I suppose . . . (**SD 25**)
6. He is supposed . . . (**SD 25**)
7. I wish you . . . (**SD 35**)
8. I'd rather he . . . (**SD 39**)
9. If I can save . . . enough money, I shall go abroad. (**SD 41**)
10. You had better . . . (**SD 43**)
11. I find him to . . . (**SD 45**)

B. Write sentences using the following words. (**SD 19**)
explain/position/me; describe/film/aunt.

C. Write these sentences again beginning each one with the words in italics: (**SD 21**)
1. He has *not only* made this mistake before, but he will make it again.
2. I realized what was happening *only then*.

D. Write the opposites of these words: (**SD 23**)
polite; agree; legible; accurate; locked; regular.

IF YOU CAN DO THIS TEST GO ON TO UNIT 2

A. Composition

a Describe the impressions of a man who returns to his home town after an absence of forty years. Expand the following into a paragraph of about 150 words:

After an absence of forty years, the man returned to the town where . . . Now, as the train drew into the station, he remembered how, as a boy, he . . . The station itself had not changed, but when . . . he got a shock. The old church which used to . . . was now surrounded by . . . He noticed with dismay that new blocks of flats had . . . After . . . , he went to his old neighbourhood. He was pleased to find that . . . Everything was exactly . . . Even the little shop where . . . He smiled with pleasure when he saw that . . . When . . . , he rapidly made his way to the house where . . .   (100 words)

b In about 200 words, describe how soldiers searched for a prisoner of war who, after escaping from his camp, had been hidden by a friendly villager. Do not write more than three paragraphs. Use the ideas given below:

Soldiers coming—the prisoner hid on the roof—saw the soldiers arrive—they questioned the villager—the villager pretended not to understand—the soldiers searched the house and fields—they got a ladder—they climbed on to the roof—the prisoner climbed down a drain-pipe—through an open window—hid in a large wardrobe—the soldiers left.

B. Key Structures
Verb-forms.

a Supply the correct form of the verbs in brackets:

Before (go) to bed, I set the alarm clock to ring at six in the morning because I wanted to get up early. It (seem) to me that I no sooner (go) to sleep than the alarm (ring). It (be) exactly 6 o'clock. After (spend) another ten minutes in bed, I (get) up and (dress). It (be) still dark when I (get) outside. There (be) no buses so I (hurry) to the station on foot. I (walk) for ten minutes when I (decide) to stop and have a cup of tea at a café which just (open). You can imagine my surprise when I (discover) that the time (be) only a quarter to six! The night before I (set) the alarm to ring an hour too soon!

b Give the correct form of the verbs in brackets:

During the past hundred years, many wonderful cave paintings (discover). Early artists (use) simple materials and (draw) on rocks. One of the first discoveries (make) in 1879 in Altamira. A young girl (walk) in a cave when she (stop) to light a candle. As soon as she (do) so, she (see) strange animals on the walls. Since then, a great many more paintings (find). In one picture, some deer (hunt) by men. The men (shoot) arrows at them and the deer (run) away. Today, we (try) to understand these pictures. Nobody (think) that they are childish. From them we (learn) a great deal about early man.

c Give the correct form of the verbs in brackets:

When the great new dam has been built it (supply) power for a third of the country's requirements. The dam (take) ten years to build and the course of the river (change). At present, twenty thousand workers (employ) and by the time the dam (complete), it (cost) millions of pounds. As many people have had to leave their homes, the government (build) new villages for them. The great dam (improve) living standards. In future, farmers (produce) more than half the country's needs; new factories (build) and the whole country (have) an adequate supply of electricity.

d Give the correct form of the verbs in brackets. Supply speech marks and arrange the conversation into paragraphs:

After the crash, two angry drivers got out of their cars. . . . you always (sleep) when you (drive)? (ask) the first driver sarcastically. You (be) on the wrong side of the road. . . . you (mean) to tell me, (shout) the second driver, that you not (notice) that this road (repair)? Of course I (drive) on the wrong side of the road when you (hit) me. The other side (be) full of holes. . . . you not (see) the traffic sign? Listen, (say) the first driver, . . . you ever (drive) a car before? I (drive) a car for twenty years. There (be) good driving schools for people like you. There they (teach) you lots of things— how to drive a car for instance. Now you really (tell) me something, (answer) the second man angrily. I happen to be a driving instructor.

e Suppose you were writing a newspaper report of the above conversation. Complete the following:

After the crash, two angry drivers got out of their cars. The first driver asked sarcastically whether the other man always . . . when he . . . He . . . on the wrong side of the road. Shouting angrily, the second driver asked the first one whether . . . He . . . on the wrong side of the road when the first man . . . him because the other side . . . full of holes. He asked him if he . . . The first driver then asked whether . . . He said that he . . . There . . . he added, good driving schools for people like the other driver. There they . . . you lots of things—how to drive a car for instance. Grateful for this information, the second man angrily informed the first one that he . . . to be a driving instructor.

f If.
Complete the following sentences:
1. If . . . you might have been knocked down by a car.
2. If . . . she will let you know.
3. If you were in my position, what . . .

g Other Verbs.
Write sentences to bring out the difference in meaning between the following pairs:
1. mustn't and needn't.   2. had to and should have.   3. have to and should.   4. must be and must eat.   5. could and was able to.   6. could and managed to.

h Complete the following:
1. On . . . he smiled with pleasure.
2. I am not looking forward to . . .
3. Instead of . . . you should see a doctor.
4. Don't you think this room needs . . .
5. You should avoid . . .

i *A* and *The*.
Supply *a(n)* or *the* where necessary in the following paragraph:
. . . editors of newspapers and . . . magazines often go to extremes to provide their readers with . . . unimportant facts and . . . statistics. Last year . . . journalist had been instructed by . . . well-known magazine to write . . . article on . . . president's palace in . . . new African republic. When . . . article arrived, . . . editor read . . . first sentence and then refused to publish it. . . . article began '. . . hundreds of . . . steps lead to . . . high wall which surrounds . . . president's palace.' . . . editor at once sent . . . journalist . . . telegram instructing him to find out . . . exact number of . . . steps and . . . height of . . . wall.

j Supply the missing words in the following sentences:
1. . . . 5 o'clock, a man . . . a small green car stopped . . . 24 Burton Road. He got . . . and walked . . . the front door of the house. He knocked . . . the door and waited. A few minutes later, the door opened and he went . . . the house.

2. I got tired . . . sitting . . . the stuffy bar, so I decided to go outside and stand . . . deck. Just as I was going . . . the bar, a tall man came up . . . me. It was Tony Adams, an old friend whom I had not seen . . . my student days. I was surprised to meet him . . . all these years.

3. A tall lady . . . black gloves . . . a long cigarette holder . . . one hand and a bag . . . the other went . . . a small, expensive shop . . . a London arcade. She stayed . . . the shop . . . hours and bought a large number of things. The assistant kept looking . . . his watch. It was a quarter to six and the shop should have shut . . . 5 o'clock, but he did not dare to ask her to leave.

4. Many people do not approve . . . blood-sports.

5. He was found guilty . . . murder and condemned . . . death.

6. Has it ever occurred . . . you that those twins are quite different . . . each other in many ways?

7. I consulted my lawyer . . . the matter and I shall act . . . his advice.

8. It is impossible to prevent them . . . quarrelling . . . each other.

9. He is responding . . . treatment and will soon be cured . . . his illness.

10. I tried to reason . . . him, but he was very rude . . . me.

11. He might be good . . . his job but you can't rely . . . him.

12. I am thinking . . . looking . . . a new job.

C. Special Difficulties

Complete the following making a sentence out of each:

1. If he happens . . .
2. It happens that . . .
3. Not only . . .
4. Never . . .
5. Seldom . . .
6. Suppose he . . .
7. I suppose you . . .
8. She is supposed . . .
9. They were supposed . . .
10. Whatever . . .
11. You can come whenever . . .
12. Whenever . . .
13. I now wish . . .
14. I wish . . . yesterday.
15. I wish . . . soon.
16. I was delighted . .
17. We are proud . . .
18. I would sooner . . .
19. He would rather not . . .
20. I would rather she . . .
21. You had better . . .
22. I find it . . .
23. No one considers him to . . .

Unit 2

INSTRUCTIONS TO THE STUDENT

In Unit 2 you will be given very little help to construct sentences in the various extended exercises you will be doing. Comprehension has been introduced as a separate exercise and is not directly related to précis writing.

Before you begin each exercise, study these instructions carefully. Read them *each time* you begin a new piece. They are very important.

How to Work—Précis

Unit 2 contains twenty passages. You will be required to write a précis of a part of each passage. Previously you were helped to find the important points. Here you must find them entirely by yourself. You will have to make a list of points and a rough draft before you write the final version of your précis.

1. Read the passage carefully two or three times. Make sure you understand it.
2. Read the instructions which will tell you where your Précis will begin and end and exactly what you will have to do. On the passage mark the places where you have to begin and end.
3. Taking great care to carry out the instructions, write a list of points *in note form*. These notes must be *brief*. Do not include any unnecessary information.
4. When joining your points, you may refer to the passage if necessary, but try to use *your own words* as far as possible. Your answer should be in one paragraph.
5. First connect your points to write a *Rough Draft* of the précis. *Do not count* the number of words until you have finished the Rough Draft.
6. In the Rough Draft, it is likely that you will go well over the word limit. Correct your Draft carefully, bringing the number of words down to the set limit. Remember that words like 'the', 'a' etc. count as single words. Words which are joined by a hyphen (e.g. 'living-room') also count as single words. You may write fewer than 80 words, but you must never write more.
7. Write a *Fair Copy* of your précis stating at the end the exact number of words you have used.
8. Neatly cross out your Points and Rough Draft.

Example

Work through this example carefully and then try to do the exercises in Unit 2 in the same way.

Christmas

As Christmas approaches, excitement mounts to a pitch. There are presents to be bought, cards to be sent, and rooms to be decorated. Parents are faced with the difficult task of concealing presents from inquisitive young children. If the gifts are large, this is sometimes a real problem. On Christmas Eve, young children
5 find the excitement almost unbearable. They are torn between the desire to go to bed early so that Santa Claus will bring their presents quickly, and the desire to stay up late in case they miss any of the fun. The desire for presents usually proves stronger. But though children go to bed early, they often lie awake for a long time, hoping to catch a glimpse of Father Christmas.
10   Last Christmas, my wife and I successfully managed to conceal a few large presents in the store-room. I was dreading the moment when my son, Jimmy,

would ask me where that new bicycle had come from, but fortunately he did not see it.

On Christmas Eve, it took the children hours to get to sleep. It must have been nearly midnight when my wife and I crept into their room and began filling stockings and pillow cases as quietly as we could. After this was done, I wheeled in the bicycle I had bought for Jimmy and left it beside the Christmas tree. We knew we would not get much sleep that night, for the children were sure to wake up early. At about five o'clock next morning, we were woken by loud sounds coming from the children's room. The children were blowing toy trumpets, banging tin drums and shouting excitedly. Before I had time to stagger out of bed, young Jimmy came sailing into the room on his brand new bicycle, and his younger sister, Elizabeth, followed close behind pushing her new pram. Even the baby arrived. He crawled into the room dragging a large balloon behind him. All of a sudden it burst. That woke us up completely. We jumped out of bed and began to play with the children. The day had really begun with a bang!

Précis

In not more than 80 words, describe what happened from the moment the writer and his wife crept into the children's room to the time when they began to play with the children. Use your own words as far as possible. Do not include anything that is not in the last paragraph.

A Possible Answer

Points (What happened)
1. Christmas Eve—crept—children's room.
2. Filled stockings, pillow cases.
3. Writer brought in bicycle.
4. Left it beside Christmas tree.
5. Early next morning woken by children.
6. Jimmy rode—parents room.
7. Sister followed—pram.
8. Baby crawled—balloon.
9. It burst.
10. Parents—out of bed.
11. Played with children.

Rough Draft (Joining the Points)
After creeping into the children's room on Christmas Eve, the writer and his wife filled stockings and pillow cases with presents. Then the writer wheeled in a bicycle which he left beside the Christmas tree. At about five o'clock next morning they were woken by loud sounds coming from the children's room. Suddenly, Jimmy rode into his parent's bedroom on his new bicycle. His sister followed him pushing her new pram. Last of all came the baby holding a large balloon. When it burst, the writer and his wife jumped out of bed and began to play with the children.   (100 words)

Fair Copy (Corrected Draft)
After creeping into the children's room on Christmas Eve, the writer and his wife not only filled stockings and pillow cases with presents, but left a bicycle beside the Christmas tree. The children woke them up very early next morning. Jimmy rode into his

parents' bedroom on his new bicycle, followed by his sister and the baby. When the balloon the baby was holding suddenly burst, the writer and his wife got up and began to play with the children.   (80 words)

Comprehension

These questions are designed to find out if you have understood the passage.
1. After you have read a question, find the answer in the passage.
2. Write a short answer *in one complete sentence* to each question. Normally, part of the question must be included in your answer.
3. Use your own words as far as possible.
4. Work neatly. Number each question carefully.

Example

Study this example carefully before attempting the comprehension exercises in Unit 2.

Comprehension

Give short answers to these questions in your own words as far as possible. Use one complete sentence for each answer.
a Why are children torn between two desires on Christmas Eve?
b Why do children often lie awake on Christmas Eve?
c Where did the writer and his wife conceal the large presents they had bought?

Possible Answers

a Children are torn between two desires on Christmas Eve because they want to go to bed early to get their presents from Santa Claus, but they also want to stay up late to see the fun.
b Children often lie awake on Christmas Eve because they hope to see Father Christmas.
c The writer and his wife hid the large presents they had bought in the store-room.

Vocabulary

You will again be asked to explain words and phrases. Here it will not be necessary to replace a word or phrase with one of your own. You must simply explain each word or phrase as it has been used in the passage.

Example

Study the example below to find out how this is done.

Vocabulary

Explain the meanings of the following words and phrases as they are used in the passage: mounts (l. 1); task (l. 3); concealing presents (l. 3); inquisitive (l. 3); catch a glimpse of (l. 9); dreading (l. 11); fortunately (l. 12).

A Possible Answer

mounts: rises.
task: job.
concealing presents: hiding gifts.
inquisitive: curious.
catch a glimpse of: see briefly.
dreading: afraid of.
fortunately: luckily.

Composition

As in the previous Unit, Composition exercises are based on ideas suggested by each passage. You will be given two types of exercise:

1. You will be provided with notes which you will be asked to expand into a plan. Your plan must contain: a title; an introduction; a development; and a conclusion. When you have made out your plan, write a composition of three or four paragraphs in about 250 words.
2. You will be provided with a plan which contains: a title; an introduction; a development; and a conclusion. You will write a composition of three or four paragraphs in about 250 words based on each plan. You are quite free to add ideas of your own or to ignore ideas that are to be found in the plan.

Examples

Here are examples of the two types of composition exercise you will be given:

1. In not more than 250 words, write an imaginary account of how the family described in the passage spent Christmas Day.
   Expand the ideas given below into a plan and provide a suitable title. Your composition should be in four paragraphs.
   Ideas: Early morning—played with children—breakfast—exchanged presents— church—home again—dinner prepared—guests arrived—excitement—more presents—dinner—Christmas party—fun and games—afternoon—sat by fire— everybody exhausted but happy.
2. In not more than 250 words, write an imaginary account of how the family described in the passage spent Christmas Day.
   Use the ideas given below. Do not write more than four paragraphs.
   Title: Christmas Day.
   Introduction: Early morning—played with children—breakfast—exchanged presents —church.
   Development: Home again—dinner prepared—guests arrived—excitement—more presents—dinner—Christmas party—fun and games.
   Conclusion: Afternoon—sat by fire—everybody exhausted but happy.

Letter-writing

Follow the instructions given under each passage.

Key Structures and Special Difficulties

When you finish the Letter-writing exercise go on to the language exercises that follow. In this Unit you will be given the opportunity to revise many of the **Key Structures** and **Special Difficulties** you learnt in *Practice and Progress*. You should refer to *Practice and Progress* if you have forgotten anything. The work you do in grammar is based on material contained in the passages. Refer to the passages frequently. They will help you to understand the grammar and to do the exercises.

Multiple Choice Questions

This is a form of comprehension test in which you are asked to choose the correct answer from a number of suggested answers. This exercise tests your ability to understand the *meaning* of the passage you have read and also to recognize grammatical errors in English.

21 Daniel Mendoza

Boxing matches were very popular in England two hundred years ago. In those days, boxers fought with bare fists for prize money. Because of this, they were
5 known as 'prize-fighters'. However, boxing was very crude, for there were no rules and a prize-fighter could be seriously injured or even killed during a match.

The two men quarrelled bitterly

One of the most colourful figures in
10 boxing history was Daniel Mendoza who was born in 1764. The use of gloves was not introduced until 1860 when the Marquis of Queensberry drew up the first set of rules. Though he was technically a
15 prize-fighter, Mendoza did much to change crude prize-fighting into a sport, for he brought science to the game. In his day, Mendoza enjoyed tremendous popularity. He was adored by rich and poor alike.

Mendoza rose to fame swiftly after a boxing-match when he was only fourteen
20 years old. This attracted the attention of Richard Humphries who was then the most eminent boxer in England. He offered to train Mendoza and his young pupil was quick to learn. In fact, Mendoza soon became so successful that Humphries turned against him. The two men quarrelled bitterly and it was clear that the argument could only be settled by a fight. A match was held at
25 Stilton where both men fought for an hour. The public bet a great deal of money on Mendoza, but he was defeated. Mendoza met Humphries in the ring on a later occasion and he lost for a second time. It was not until his third match in 1790 that he finally beat Humphries and became Champion of England. Meanwhile, he founded a highly successful Academy and even Lord Byron became
30 one of his pupils. He earned enormous sums of money and was paid as much as £100 for a single appearance. Despite this, he was so extravagant that he was always in debt. After he was defeated by a boxer called Gentleman Jackson, he was quickly forgotten. He was sent to prison for failing to pay his debts and died in poverty in 1836.

Comprehension

Give short answers to these questions in your own words as far as possible. Use one complete sentence for each answer.
a Why were boxers known as 'prize-fighters' two hundred years ago?
b Why was boxing very crude in those days?
c What was Mendoza's chief contribution to boxing?

Vocabulary

Explain the meanings of the following words and phrases as they are used in the passage: bare (l. 3); injured (l. 8); drew up (l. 13); crude (l. 16); enjoyed tremendous popularity (ll. 17–18); adored (l. 18); alike (l. 18).

Précis

In not more than 80 words write a brief account of Mendoza's career from the time he quarrelled with Humphries. Use your own words as far as possible. Do not include anything that is not in the last paragraph.

Composition

In not more than 250 words, write an imaginary account of the first fight between Mendoza and Humphries. Expand the ideas given below into a plan and provide a suitable title. Your composition should be in four paragraphs.

Ideas: The quarrel—Mendoza and Humphries: bets from supporters—atmosphere just before the fight—the fight itself—Mendoza's defeat—effect on him and his supporters.

Letter-writing

On a full page, show the exact position of each of the following:
The address and date; the beginning of the letter; the Introduction; the Purpose; the Conclusion; the letter-ending; the signature; the postscript. Supply all necessary full stops and commas.

Key Structures and Special Difficulties

Exercises

1. *Boxing matches were very popular in England two hundred years ago.* (ll. 1–2.) Write two sentences using the words *ago* and *before*. (1 **KS 97b**)
2. *a prize fighter could be seriously injured* (ll. 7–8). Write two sentences using *could* and *was able to* (1 **KS 107c**)
3. *The use of gloves was not introduced until 1860.* (ll. 11–12). Write a sentence using the construction *not . . . until.* (1 **KS 29d**)
4. *He was adored by rich and poor alike.* (l. 18.) Note the use of *by* in this sentence. Write two sentences using *by* in the same way. (1 **KS 89**)
5. *Mendoza rose to fame.* (l. 19.) Write two sentences illustrating the use of *rose* and *raised.* (1 **SD 132a**)
6. *his young pupil was quick to learn* (ll. 21–22). Write two sentences using the following: *pleased to* and *sorry to* (**SD 37**)
7. *it was clear* (ll. 23–24). Write three sentences bringing out the different meanings of the word *clear*. Write a sentence using the word *clean*. (1 **SD 202c**)
8. *He was sent to prison for failing to pay his debts.* (l. 33.) Note the form of the verb *fail* here. Write sentences using a verb after each of the following: afraid of; without; apologize for; congratulate on. (1 **KS 51**)

Multiple Choice Questions

a Choose the one answer (A, B, C or D) which you think is correct in the following:
Mendoza was sent to prison because:

A   he was extravagant;
B   he owed money and couldn't pay it;
C   he was often in debt;
D   he was defeated by Gentleman Jackson.

b Choose the two answers which you think are correct in the following:
Mendoza's . . . to fame was noted by Richard Humphries.

A rise   B rose   C raise   D claim   E rising

22 By Heart

Some plays are so successful that they run for years on end. In many ways, this is unfortunate for the poor actors who are required to go on repeating the same lines
5 night after night. One would expect them to know their parts by heart and never have cause to falter. Yet this is not always the case.

A famous actor in a highly successful
10 play was once cast in the role of an aristocrat who had been imprisoned in the Bastille for twenty years. In the last act, a gaoler would always come on to the stage with a letter which he would
15 hand to the prisoner. Even though the noble was expected to read the letter at

'*The light is indeed dim, sire*'

each performance, he always insisted that it should be written out in full.
   One night, the gaoler decided to play a joke on his colleague to find out if, after so many performances, he had managed to learn the contents of the letter
20 by heart. The curtain went up on the final act of the play and revealed the aristocrat sitting alone behind bars in his dark cell. Just then, the gaoler appeared with the precious letter in his hands. He entered the cell and presented the letter to the aristocrat. But the copy he gave him had not been written out in full as usual. It was simply a blank sheet of paper. The gaoler looked on eagerly,
25 anxious to see if his fellow-actor had at last learnt his lines. The noble stared at the blank sheet of paper for a few seconds. Then, squinting his eyes, he said: 'The light is dim. Read the letter to me.' And he promptly handed the sheet of paper to the gaoler. Finding that he could not remember a word of the letter either, the gaoler replied: 'The light is indeed dim, sire. I must get my glasses.'
30 With this, he hurried off the stage. Much to the aristocrat's amusement, the gaoler returned a few moments later with a pair of glasses and the usual copy of the letter which he proceeded to read to the prisoner.

Comprehension

Give short answers to these questions in your own words as far as possible. Use one complete sentence for each answer.
a Why are actors in successful plays in many ways unfortunate?
b In which act of the play was the aristocrat given a letter to read?
c Why did the gaoler decide to play a joke on the aristocrat?

Vocabulary

Explain the meanings of the following words and phrases as they are used in the passage: run (l. 2); on end (l. 2); are required (ll. 3–4); repeating (l. 4); falter (l. 7); role (l. 10); hand (l. 15); in full (l. 17).

62

Winking —one eye close

Précis

In not more than 80 words describe what happened after the curtain went up on the final act of the play. Use your own words as far as possible. Do not include anything that is not in the last paragraph.

Composition

Write a composition of about 250 words using the ideas given below. Do not write more than four paragraphs.

Title: Six Short Weeks.

Introduction: A new play called 'The World Tomorrow' to be shown. Highly advertised—public interest—cast of famous actors.

Development: First night—play not well-received—supposed to be funny—nobody laughed—people walked out—bad reviews.

Conclusion: The play ran for six weeks—last performance—small audience—actors struggled through—the audience found the last line of the play very funny: 'Our six short weeks have hastened to their end.' Even the actors laughed.

Letter-writing

Write five sentences which could be used to begin a letter and five sentences which could be used to end one.

Key Structures and Special Difficulties

1. *Some plays are so successful that they run for years on end.* (ll. 1–2.) Write three sentences illustrating the use of *so . . . that*; *such . . . that*; and *such a . . . that*. (**1 SD 92**)
2. *In the last act, a gaoler would always come on to the stage.* (ll. 12–14.) Which verb could be used in place of *would* here? Write two sentences illustrating the use of *would* and *used to.* (**1 KS 139b**)
3. *The noble was expected to read the letter at each performance. He always insisted that it should be written out in full.* (ll. 15–17.) Join these two sentences, then compare your answer with the sentence in the passage. (**1 KS 127**)
4. *He always insisted that it should be written out in full.* (l. 17.) Write sentences using the following: He suggested that . . . He insisted that . . . He demanded that . . . (**1 KS 155**)
5. *He had managed to learn the contents of the letter by heart.* (ll. 19–20.) Write two sentences showing how *managed to* can be used as the opposite of *could not.* (**1 KS 163** Exercise C)
6. *He entered the cell. He presented the letter to the aristocrat.* (ll. 22–23.) Join these two sentences, then compare your answer with the sentence in the passage. (**1 KS 71**)
7. *The noble stared at the blank sheet of paper.* (ll. 25–26.) Write sentences using the verbs *throw at* and *point at* (**1 KS 87e**)
8. *I must get my glasses.* (l. 29.) Which verb can we use in place of *must* here? (**1 KS 45a**)

Multiple Choice Questions

a Choose the one answer (A, B, C or D) which you think is correct in the following:

What did the aristocrat always expect to receive from the gaoler?

A   A blank sheet of paper.
B   A pair of glasses.
C   A letter written out in full.
D   A letter not written out in full.

b Choose the two answers which you think are correct in the following:
The gaoler . . . get his glasses because the light was dim.

A   should   B   should have   C   had to   D   was obliged to   E   must

23   One Man's Meat is Another Man's Poison

People become quite illogical when they
try to decide what can be eaten and what
cannot be eaten. If you lived in the
Mediterranean, for instance, you would
5   consider octopus a great delicacy. You
would not be able to understand why
some people find it repulsive. On the
other hand, your stomach would turn at
the idea of frying potatoes in animal fat—
10   the normally accepted practice in many
northern countries. The sad truth is that
most of us have been brought up to eat
certain foods and we stick to them all our
lives.

... *would consider octopus a
great delicacy*

15   No creature has received more praise
and abuse than the common garden snail.
Cooked in wine, snails are a great luxury in various parts of the world. There
are countless people who, ever since their early years, have learned to associate
snails with food. My friend, Robert, lives in a country where snails are despised.
20   As his flat is in a large town, he has no garden of his own. For years he has been
asking me to collect snails from my garden and take them to him. The idea
never appealed to me very much, but one day, after a heavy shower, I happened
to be walking in my garden when I noticed a huge number of snails taking a
stroll on some of my prize plants. Acting on a sudden impulse, I collected
25   several dozen, put them in a paper bag, and took them to Robert. Robert was
delighted to see me and equally pleased with my little gift. I left the bag in the
hall and Robert and I went into the living-room where we talked for a couple
of hours. I had forgotten all about the snails when Robert suddenly said that I
must stay to dinner. Snails would, of course, be the main dish. I did not fancy
30   the idea and I reluctantly followed Robert out of the room. To our dismay, we
saw that there were snails everywhere: they had escaped from the paper bag
and had taken complete possession of the hall! I have never been able to look
at a snail since then.

Comprehension

Give short answers to these questions in your own words as far as possible. Use one
complete sentence for each answer.
a In what part of the world is octopus considered a great delicacy?
b Why do we stick to certain foods all our lives?
c Why did the writer's friend find it difficult to obtain snails?

Vocabulary

Explain the meanings of the following words and phrases as they are used in the
passage: illogical (l. 1); instance (l. 4); repulsive (l. 7); stick (l. 13); various (l. 17);
associate (l. 18); appealed to (l. 22).

64

Précis

In not more than 80 words describe what happened from the moment the writer collected snails from his garden. Use your own words as far as possible. Do not include anything that is not in the last paragraph.

Composition

In not more than 250 words write a continuation of the passage. Expand the ideas given below into a plan and provide a suitable title. Your composition should be in three or four paragraphs.
Ideas : Snails—walls, ceiling—coat pockets—effort to collect them—ladders etc.—marks everywhere—Robert amused—cooked the snails—a meal for one.

Letter-writing

In not more than 100 words write a letter of three paragraphs inviting a friend to spend a week-end with your family at your home in the country.

Key Structures and Special Difficulties

Exercises

1. *People become quite illogical when* . . . (l. 1). Write two sentences illustrating the use of the words *quite* and *quiet*. (**1 SD 136b**)
2. *If you lived in the Mediterranean, you would consider octopus a great delicacy.* (ll. 3–5.) Write this sentence again beginning 'If you had lived . . .' (**1 KS 158b**)
3. *the normally accepted practice* (l. 10). Write two sentences using the words *practice* and *practise*. (**1 SD 168a**)
4. *The sad truth is that most of us* . . . (ll. 11–12). Write two sentences using *most* and *the most*. (**1 KS 138d**)
5. *There are countless people who ever since their earliest years* . . . (ll. 17–18). Write three sentences using the words *since, for* and *ago*. (**1 KS 80**)
6. *As his flat is in a large town* . . . (l. 20). What does *as* mean in this sentence? Write three sentences illustrating the other meaning of *as*. (**1 SD 46a**)
7. *For years he has been asking me to collect snails.* (ll. 20–21.) Write two sentences using *has been asking* and *has asked*. (**1 KS 133**)
8. *I happened to be walking in my garden.* (ll. 22–23.) Write sentences using the following: *he happens, it happened that, happened.* (**SD 17a**)

Multiple Choice Questions

a Choose the one answer (A, B, C or D) which you think is correct in the following:
The writer put the snails in a paper bag:

A in case they escaped;
B to prevent them from escaping;
C to take them to his friend Robert;
D because they were strolling on his prize plants.

b Choose the two answers which you think are correct in each of the following:
  1. *The writer and his friend went out of the living-room* . . . *get the snails.*

  A in order that B to C in order to D so that E for

  2. *They felt* . . . *when they noticed that the snails had escaped.*

  A disappointed B unhappy C pleased D sad E angry

24   A Skeleton in the Cupboard

We often read in novels how a seemingly respectable person or family has some terrible secret which has been concealed from strangers for years. The English
5 language possesses a vivid saying to describe this sort of situation. The terrible secret is called 'a skeleton in the cupboard'. At some dramatic moment in the story, the terrible secret becomes known
10 and a reputation is ruined. The reader's hair stands on end when he reads in the final pages of the novel that the heroine, a dear old lady who had always been so kind to everybody, had, in her youth,
15 poisoned every one of her five husbands.

. . . *some terrible secret*

It is all very well for such things to occur in fiction. To varying degrees, we all have secrets which we do not want even our closest friends to learn, but few of us have skeletons in the cupboard. The only person I know who has a skeleton in the cupboard is George Carlton,
20 and he is very proud of the fact. George studied medicine in his youth. Instead of becoming a doctor, however, he became a successful writer of detective stories. I once spent an uncomfortable week-end which I shall never forget at his house. George showed me to the guest-room which, he said, was rarely used. He told me to unpack my things and then come down to dinner. After I had stacked my
25 shirts and underclothes in two empty drawers, I decided to hang in the cupboard one of the two suits I had brought with me. I opened the cupboard door and then stood in front of it petrified. A skeleton was dangling before my eyes. The sudden movement of the door made it sway slightly and it gave me the impression that it was about to leap out at me. Dropping my suit, I dashed downstairs to tell
30 George. This was worse than 'a terrible secret'; this was a *real* skeleton! But George was unsympathetic. 'Oh, that,' he said with a smile as if he were talking about an old friend. 'That's Sebastian. You forget that I was a medical student once upon a time.'

Comprehension

Give short answers to these questions in your own words as far as possible. Use one complete sentence for each answer.
a Explain the saying 'a skeleton in the cupboard'.
b What was the terrible secret of the dear old lady who had always been so kind to everybody?
c What does George Carlton do for a living?

Vocabulary

Explain the meanings of the following words and phrases as they are used in the passage: seemingly (l. 1); concealed (l. 3); vivid saying (l. 5); reputation (l. 10); ruined (l. 10); fiction (l. 17); to varying degrees (l. 17).

Précis

In not more than 80 words describe the writer's experiences from the moment he was shown to the guest-room. Use your own words as far as possible. Do not include anything that is not in the last paragraph.

Composition

In not more than 250 words write a continuation of the above passage in the first person. Use the ideas given below. Do not write more than four paragraphs.

Title : A Week-end with Sebastian.
Introduction : George Carlton refused to remove skeleton—nowhere to put it.
Development : How I spent the night—very uncomfortable—took Sebastian out of the cupboard—walked around the house with him looking for somewhere to put him— maid just going to bed—saw Sebastian walking around—screamed—Carlton appeared —the scene.
Conclusion : Two years later I read about myself and Sebastian in one of Carlton's detective stories.

Letter-writing

In not more than 100 words write a letter of three paragraphs to your family doctor (who is also a personal friend) telling him that you have not been feeling well lately and asking him if you could make an appointment.

Key Structures and Special Difficulties

Exercises

1. *We often read in novels . . .* (l. 1). Note the position of *often* here. Write similar sentences using the words *frequently, rarely, always* and *never*. (1 **KS 15** Exercise B)
2. *we do not want even our closest friends to learn* (ll. 17–18). Note this pattern. Write two sentences in the same way using the verbs *teach* and *allow*. (1 **SD 34a**)
3. *few of us have skeletons in the cupboard* (l. 18). Write sentences illustrating the difference between: *few* and *a few*; *little* and *a little*. (1 **KS 86b**)
4. *he is very proud of the fact* (l. 20). Which words normally follow these words: aware, ready, patient, afraid, fortunate, curious, dependent, different, skilful, familiar and close. (1 **KS 170**)
5. *The sudden movement of the door made it sway.* (ll. 27–28.) Note this use of *make*. Write two sentences using *make* and *let*. (1 **SD 144**)
6. *'Oh, that,' he said . . .* (l. 31). Note this use of speech marks. (1 **SD 74**) Write this piece of conversation again using speech marks:
   You must see Arsenic and Old Lace again Tom said. It's a wonderful film. No thank you I answered. I don't think I could stand it. I saw it years ago said Tom. I shall never forget those dear old ladies. And I shall never forget that dreadful moment when Boris Karloff suddenly appeared at the window I said. I nearly jumped out of my seat.

Multiple Choice Questions

Choose the one answer (A, B, C or D) which you think is correct in the following:
When the writer described his experiences to George :

A   George didn't feel sorry for him;
B   George behaved in an unpleasant manner;
C   George wasn't upset;
D   George said he didn't like the writer.

25 The 'Cutty Sark'

One of the most famous sailing ships of the nineteenth century, the *Cutty Sark*, can still be seen at Greenwich. She stands on dry land and is visited by
5 thousands of people each year. She serves as an impressive reminder of the great ships of the past. Before they were replaced by steam-ships, sailing vessels like the *Cutty Sark* were used to carry
10 tea from China and wool from Australia. The *Cutty Sark* was one of the fastest sailing ships that has ever been built. The only other ship to match her was the *Thermopylae*. Both these ships set out
15 from Shanghai on June 18th, 1872 on an exciting race to England. This race,

A temporary rudder was made

which went on for exactly four months, was the last of its kind. It marked the end of the great tradition of ships with sails and the beginning of a new era.

The first of the two ships to reach Java after the race had begun was the
20 *Thermopylae*, but on the Indian Ocean, the *Cutty Sark* took the lead. It seemed certain that she would be the first ship home, but during the race she had a lot of bad luck. In August, she was struck by a very heavy storm during which her rudder was torn away. The *Cutty Sark* rolled from side to side and it became impossible to steer her. A temporary rudder was made on board from spare
25 planks and it was fitted with great difficulty. This greatly reduced the speed of the ship, for there was danger that if she travelled too quickly, this rudder would be torn away as well. Because of this, the *Cutty Sark* lost her lead. After crossing the equator, the captain called in at a port to have a new rudder fitted, but by now the *Thermopylae* was over five hundred miles ahead. Though the
30 new rudder was fitted at tremendous speed, it was impossible for the *Cutty Sark* to win. She arrived in England a week after the *Thermopylae*. Even this was remarkable, considering that she had had so many delays. There is no doubt that if she had not lost her rudder she would have won the race easily.

Comprehension

Give short answers to these questions in your own words as far as possible. Use one complete sentence for each answer.
a Where can the *Cutty Sark* be seen?
b What sort of cargo did ships like the *Cutty Sark* carry?
c How long did the race between the *Cutty Sark* and the *Thermopylae* last?

Vocabulary

Explain the meanings of the following words and phrases as they are used in the passage: reminder (l. 6); match (l. 13); era (l. 18); struck (l. 22); steer (l. 24); temporary (l. 24); on board (l. 24).

Précis

In not more than 80 words write an account of the race between the *Cutty Sark* and the *Thermopylae* after they set out from Shanghai. Use your own words as far as possible. Do not include anything that is not in the last paragraph.

Composition

In not more than 250 words write a composition entitled 'Ships of the Past'. Expand the ideas given below into a plan.
Ideas : Ancient ships—oars—galley slaves—Viking ships—Eric the Red—early sailing ships—Columbus—galleons—the Spanish Armada—warships—Nelson—the coming of steam—the *Great Eastern*.

Letter-writing

Imagine you are at present travelling on a ship. Write a letter in three paragraphs of about 100 words to your parents describing your journey so far.

Key Structures and Special Difficulties

Exercises

1. *vessels like the* Cutty Sark *were used to carry tea* (ll. 8–10). Write three sentences using the following: *I use, I am used to, I used to.* (1 **SD 140a**)
2. *The* Cutty Sark *was one of the fastest sailing ships.* (ll. 11–12.) Write sentences using the words *fast* and *faster than.* (1 **KS 27**)
3. *these ships set out from Shanghai* (ll. 14–15). Write two sentences using the verbs *set off* and *set up.* (1 **SD 36b**)
4. *This race . . . was the last of its kind.* (ll. 16–17.) Write two sentences using *its* and *it's.* (1 **SD 52b**)
5. *she had a lot of bad luck* (ll. 21–22). Write sentences using *a lot of, a great many* and *a great deal of.* (1 **KS 141b**)
6. *A temporary rudder was made on board.* (l. 24.) Which of the following words are preceded by *on* (1 **SD 200**) and which by *in* (**SD 15**): fire, ink, common, tears, foot, purpose, love, a hurry.
7. *if she travelled too quickly* (l. 26). Write two sentences showing the difference between *very* and *too.* (1 **SD 80c**)
8. *The captain called in at a port to have a new rudder fitted.* (l. 28.) Note this use of *have.* (1 **KS 161**) Write these sentences again using *have* with the verbs in italics:
   He *is building* a house.
   She *has cleaned* his suit.
9. *it was impossible for the* Cutty Sark *to win* (ll. 30–31). Write two sentences using the verbs *win* and *beat.* (1 **SD 132c**)

Multiple Choice Questions

Choose the two answers which you think are correct in each of the following:

1. *The* Cutty Sark *had to travel slowly . . . her temporary rudder.*

A because she lost B if she lost C without D in case she lost E lest she lose

2. *With her original rudder it is . . . she would have won the race.*

A unlikely B improbable C certain D sure E doubtless

26 Wanted: a Large Biscuit Tin

No one can avoid being influenced by advertisements. Much as we may pride ourselves on our good taste, we are no longer free to choose the things we want,
5 for advertising exerts a subtle influence on us. In their efforts to persuade us to buy this or that product, advertisers have made a close study of human nature and have classified all our little weaknesses.
10 Advertisers discovered years ago that all of us love to get something for nothing. An advertisement which begins with the magic word FREE can rarely go wrong. These days, advertisers not only offer
15 free samples, but free cars, free houses, and free trips round the world as well.

a biscuit on a wheelbarrow

They devise hundreds of competitions which will enable us to win huge sums of money. Radio and television have made it possible for advertisers to capture the attention of millions of people in this way.
20 During a radio programme, a company of biscuit manufacturers once asked listeners to bake biscuits and send them to their factory. They offered to pay $2 a pound for the biggest biscuit baked by a listener. The response to this competition was tremendous. Before long, biscuits of all shapes and sizes began arriving at the factory. One lady brought in a biscuit on a wheelbarrow. It
25 weighed nearly 500 pounds. A little later, a man came along with a biscuit which occupied the whole boot of his car. All the biscuits that were sent were carefully weighed. The largest was 713 pounds. It seemed certain that this would win the prize. But just before the competition closed, a lorry arrived at the factory with a truly colossal biscuit which weighed 2400 pounds. It had
30 been baked by a college student who had used over 1000 pounds of flour, 800 pounds of sugar, 200 pounds of fat, and 400 pounds of various other ingredients. It was so heavy that a crane had to be used to remove it from the lorry. The manufacturers had to pay more money than they had anticipated, for they bought the biscuit from the student for $4800.

Comprehension

Give short answers to these questions in your own words as far as possible. Use one complete sentence for each answer.
a Why are we no longer free to choose the things we want?
b Why have advertisers made a close study of human weaknesses?
c How can advertisers capture the attention of millions of people?

Vocabulary

Explain the meanings of the following words and phrases as they are used in the passage: no longer (ll. 3–4); in their efforts to persuade us (l. 6); classified (l. 9); free (l. 13); enable (l. 17); capture (l. 18).

70

Précis

In not more than 80 words write an account of the competition organized by a company of biscuit manufacturers. Use your own words as far as possible. Do not include anything that is not in the last paragraph.

Composition

In not more than 250 words describe a radio show organized by a firm of soap manufacturers. Use the ideas given below and provide a suitable title. Do not write more than two paragraphs.

Introduction : A member of the audience will be asked a maximum of ten questions. Each time he answers a question correctly, he may accept a money prize or ask for a more difficult question. The minimum prize is £2 for a correct answer to the first question. This goes on doubling itself, reaching a maximum of £2,048 for ten correct answers.

Development and Conclusion: Man being questioned in front of audience—questions of all types (e.g. spelling difficult words, general knowledge etc.). Excitement mounts up as man answers question after question until he reaches the last one.

Letter-writing

Write a letter of about 100 words in three paragraphs informing a friend of yours that you will be moving into his neighbourhood. Ask him to help you to find accommodation.

Key Structures and Special Difficulties

Exercises

1. *No one can avoid being influenced by advertisements.* (ll. 1–2.) Complete the following:
   (1 KS 166)
   He enjoys . . .
   Fancy . . .
   It's no use . . .
   It's not worth . . .
   Would you mind . . .
2. *can rarely go wrong* (l. 13). Write sentences using the following: go bad; turn yellow; grow quiet. (1 SD 190)
3. *in this way* (l. 19). Write sentences to bring out the correct meaning of each of the following: *in the way, on the way,* and *by the way.* (1 SD 22a)
4. *. . . and send them to their factory* (l. 21). Note this pattern. Write similar sentences using the verbs *lend* and *give.* (1 SD 18)
5. *One lady brought in a biscuit* (l. 24). Write two sentences showing the difference between *one* and *a.* (1 SD 86)
6. *It was heavy. A crane had to be used to remove it from the lorry.* (l. 32.) Join these two sentences then compare your answer with the sentence in the passage. (1 SD 92)

Multiple Choice Questions

Choose the one answer (A, B, C or D) which you think is correct in the following:
In the competition rules it was stated that the winner would be paid :

A   according to the size of the biscuit he baked;
B   according to the weight of the cake he baked;
C   according to the cost of the cake he baked;
D   according to the weight of the biscuit he baked.

27   Nothing to Sell and Nothing to Buy

It has been said that everyone lives by
selling something. In the light of this
statement, teachers live by selling knowledge, philosophers by selling wisdom
5 and priests by selling spiritual comfort.
Though it may be possible to measure
the value of material goods in terms of
money, it is extremely difficult to estimate
the true value of the services which people
10 perform for us. There are times when we
would willingly give everything we
possess to save our lives, yet we might
grudge paying a surgeon a high fee for
offering us precisely this service. The
15 conditions of society are such that skills
have to be paid for in the same way that
goods are paid for at a shop. Everyone has something to sell.

. . . freedom from care

Tramps seem to be the only exception to this general rule. Beggars almost sell
themselves as human beings to arouse the pity of passers-by. But real tramps are
20 not beggars. They have nothing to sell and require nothing from others. In
seeking independence, they do not sacrifice their human dignity. A tramp may
ask you for money, but he will never ask you to feel sorry for him. He has
deliberately chosen to lead the life he leads and is fully aware of the consequences.
He may never be sure where the next meal is coming from, but he is free from
25 the thousands of anxieties which afflict other people. His few material possessions
make it possible for him to move from place to place with ease. By having to
sleep in the open, he gets far closer to the world of nature than most of us ever
do. He may hunt, beg, or steal occasionally to keep himself alive; he may even,
in times of real need, do a little work; but he will never sacrifice his freedom.
30 We often speak of tramps with contempt and put them in the same class as
beggars, but how many of us can honestly say that we have not felt a little
envious of their simple way of life and their freedom from care?

Comprehension

Give short answers to these questions in your own words as far as possible. Use one
complete sentence for each answer.
a Which of the two is it easier to estimate in terms of money: the value of material
goods or the value of services?
b How do beggars arouse the pity of passers-by?
c How do tramps differ from beggars?

Vocabulary

Explain the meanings of the following words and phrases as they are used in the
passage: value (l. 7); estimate (l. 8); perform (l. 10); possess (l. 12); grudge (l. 13);
precisely (l. 14); skills (l. 15).

Précis

In not more than 80 words give an account of a tramp's way of life. Use your own words as far as possible. Do not include anything that is not in the last paragraph.

Composition

In not more than 250 words write an answer to the above passage criticizing a tramp's way of life. Expand the ideas given below into a plan and provide a suitable title. Your composition should be in four paragraphs.

Ideas: Tramps—free, but freedom paid for by others—selfish way of life—unwillingness to assume responsibility for others (home, children, work etc.)—lazy parasites on society—if we had the mentality of tramps, we would still be savages.

Letter-writing

Write a letter of about 100 words in three paragraphs to a relation who lives abroad. Ask him whether it would be possible for you to get a job abroad for a few months to help to pay for a holiday you intend to have.

Key Structures and Special Difficulties

Exercises

1. *It has been said that . . .* (l. 1). Write two sentences using the following: *He is said . . ., It is said that . . .* (1 **KS 146b**)
2. *teachers live by selling knowledge* (ll. 3–4). Write sentences using the following words: *information, news, work* and *luggage.* (1 **KS 138a**)
3. *There are times . . .* (l. 10). Write sentences using the following: *it will be; there was; there has been.* (1 **SD 58**)
4. *we would willingly give everything we possess to save our lives* (ll. 10–12). Note the use of *to* here. Write sentences using the following: *so as not to; in order that my mother; so that.* (1 **SD 148**)
5. *skills have to be paid for* (ll. 15–16). Write two sentences using the following: *to be found; to be sold.* (1 **KS 89**)
6. *He may never be sure where the next meal is coming from.* (l. 24.) Write these sentences again changing the position of the words in italics. Where possible omit the words *whom* and *which.* (**SD 13**)
   By whom was this book written?
   This is not the sort of book *in* which I am interested.
7. *He has to sleep in the open. He gets far closer to the world of nature than most of us ever do.* (ll. 26–27.) Join these two sentences then compare your answer with the sentence in the passage. (1 **KS 51**)

Multiple Choice Questions

a Choose the one answer (A, B, C or D) which you think is correct in the following:
What makes it possible for a tramp to move easily from one place to another?

A The fact that he doesn't own very many things;
B The fact that he doesn't have to work;
C The fact that he can always get a lift in a car;
D The fact that he hasn't a fixed address.

b Choose the two answers which you think are correct in the following:
We must admire tramps for their determination . . . lose their freedom.

A not to   B to not   C to don't   D to ever   E never to

28 A Pound too Dear

Small boats loaded with wares sped to the
great liner as she was entering the harbour. Before she had anchored, the men
from the boats had climbed on board and
5 the decks were soon covered with colourful rugs from Persia, silks from India,
copper coffee pots, and beautiful hand-
made silver-ware. It was difficult not to
be tempted. Many of the tourists on
10 board had begun bargaining with the
tradesmen, but I decided not to buy
anything until I had disembarked.

colourful rugs from Persia

I had no sooner got off the ship than I
was assailed by a man who wanted to sell
15 me a diamond ring. I had no intention of
buying one, but I could not conceal the
fact that I was impressed by the size of the diamonds. Some of them were as big
as marbles. The man went to great lengths to prove that the diamonds were real.
As we were walking past a shop, he held a diamond firmly against the window
20 and made a deep impression in the glass. It took me over half an hour to get rid
of him.

The next man to approach me was selling expensive pens and watches. I
examined one of the pens closely. It certainly looked genuine. At the base of the
gold cap, the words 'made in the U.S.A.' had been neatly inscribed. The man
25 said that the pen was worth £10, but as a special favour, he would let me have it
for £8. I shook my head and held up a finger indicating that I was willing to
pay a pound. Gesticulating wildly, the man acted as if he found my offer outrageous, but he eventually reduced the price to £3. Shrugging my shoulders, I
began to walk away when, a moment later, he ran after me and thrust the pen
30 into my hands. Though he kept throwing up his arms in despair, he readily
accepted the pound I gave him. I felt especially pleased with my wonderful
bargain—until I got back to the ship. No matter how hard I tried, it was impossible to fill this beautiful pen with ink and to this day it has never written a
single word!

Comprehension

Give short answers to these questions in your own words as far as possible. Use one
complete sentence for each answer.
a What happened as the great liner was entering the harbour?
b Why was the writer impressed by the size of the diamonds?
c What did the diamond-seller do to prove that his diamonds were real?

Vocabulary

Explain the meanings of the following words and phrases as they are used in the
passage: loaded with wares (l. 1); liner (l. 2); rugs (l. 6); bargaining (l. 10); went to
great lengths (l. 18); impression (l. 20); to get rid of him (ll. 20–21).

74

Précis

In not more than 80 words describe the writer's experiences after he had got rid of the diamond-seller. Use your own words as far as possible. Do not include anything that is not in the last paragraph.

Composition

In not more than 250 words write an imaginary account, mainly in dialogue form, of the scene that took place between the writer and the man who sold him the pen. Use the ideas given below.

Title: The Bargain.

Introduction: Man approached with pens and watches—held them up—writer showed interest.

Development and Conclusion: Writer asked to see a pen—man handed him one—argument about the price—gradually reduced to £3—writer walked away—man followed—made it clear that he was being robbed but accepted £1. Writer pleased, but man disappeared quickly.

Letter-writing

You have heard that a friend of yours wishes to sell his tape-recorder. Write him a letter of about 100 words in three paragraphs. Express interest in the machine and ask him to tell you about its condition and how much he wants.

Key Structures and Special Difficulties

Exercises

1. *I had no sooner got off the ship than I* . . . (l. 13). Join these pairs of sentences with *no sooner . . . than.* (**1 SD 98a**)
   I opened the door. The telephone began to ring.
   He finished his speech. Everyone began to clap.
2. *Some of them were as big as marbles.* (ll. 17–18.) Write two sentences illustrating the use of *as . . . as* and *not as . . . as.* (**1 KS 86a**)
3. *As we were walking past a shop* . . . (l. 19). Complete the following sentences: (**1 KS 25**)
   While I was working in the garden . . .
   I was just going into the shop when . . .
4. *It took me over half an hour to get rid of him.* (ll. 20–21.) Write two sentences using *it takes* and *it has taken.* (**1 SD 130c**)
5. *'made in the U.S.A.'* (l. 24). Write sentences using each of the following: *made in, made by, made of* and *made from.* (**1 SD 32a**)
6. *to this day it has never written a word* (ll. 33–34). Write two sentences using the phrases *up till now* and *so far.* (**1 KS 77**)

Multiple Choice Questions

Choose the two answers which you think are correct in each of the following:

1. *It was impossible to fill the pen with ink* . . . *I tried very hard.*

   A if   B provided that   C though   D not only   E even if

2. *The man was very* . . . *to accept the pound I gave him.*

   A glad   B reluctant   C unwilling   D pleased   E sorry

29 Funny or Not?

Whether we find a joke funny or not largely depends on where we have been brought up. The sense of humour is mysteriously bound up with national
5 characteristics. A Frenchman, for instance, might find it hard to laugh at a Russian joke. In the same way, a Russian might fail to see anything amusing in a joke which would make an Englishman
10 laugh to tears.

Most funny stories are based on comic situations. In spite of national differences, certain funny situations have a universal appeal. No matter where you live, you
15 would find it difficult not to laugh at, say, Charlie Chaplin's early films. However, a

a Russian might fail to see anything amusing

new type of humour, which stems largely from America, has recently come into fashion. It is called 'sick humour'. Comedians base their jokes on tragic situations like violent death or serious accidents. Many people find this sort of joke dis-
20 tasteful. The following example of 'sick humour' will enable you to judge for yourself.

A man who had broken his right leg was taken to hospital a few weeks before Christmas. From the moment he arrived there, he kept on pestering his doctor to tell him when he would be able to go home. He dreaded having to spend
25 Christmas in hospital. Though the doctor did his best, the patient's recovery was slow. On Christmas day, the man still had his right leg in plaster. He spent a miserable day in bed thinking of all the fun he was missing. The following day, however, the doctor consoled him by telling him that his chances of being able to leave hospital in time for New Year celebrations were good. The man took
30 heart and, sure enough, on New Year's Eve he was able to hobble along to a party. To compensate for his unpleasant experiences in hospital, the man drank a little more than was good for him. In the process, he enjoyed himself thoroughly and kept telling everybody how much he hated hospitals. He was still mumbling something about hospitals at the end of the party when he slipped on a piece of
35 ice and broke his left leg.

Comprehension

Give short answers to these questions in your own words as far as possible. Use one complete sentence for each answer.
a Why might a Frenchman find it hard to laugh at a Russian joke?
b Why do people all over the world find Charlie Chaplin's early films amusing?
c Where did 'sick humour' originate?

Vocabulary

Explain the meanings of the following words and phrases as they are used in the passage: brought up (l. 3); mysteriously bound up with (l. 4); make (l. 9); universal appeal (ll. 13–14); stems (l. 17); come into fashion (ll. 17–18); distasteful (ll. 19–20).

Précis

Relate the story told in the passage *in not more than 80 words*. Use your own words as far as possible. Do not include anything that is not in the last paragraph.

Composition

In not more than 250 words tell a funny story you know well. Make out a full plan and provide a suitable title. Your composition should be in three or four paragraphs.

Letter-writing

You cannot find your overcoat and think you may have left it at the house of a friend whom you visited recently. Write him a letter of about 100 words in three paragraphs asking him if you did in fact leave your overcoat at his house.

Key Structures and Special Difficulties

Exercises

1. *depends on* (l. 2). Which words normally follow these verbs: operate, differ, smell, encourage, lean, approve, delight, suffer, assure, escape, interested, concentrate, include. (**1 KS 55**)
2. *A Frenchman ... might find it hard to laugh at a Russian joke.* (ll. 5–7.) Note this pattern. Write similar sentences using the following: *He found it ...*; *She considered it ...*; *He thought it ...* (**1 SD 208**)
3. *to laugh at a Russian joke* (ll. 6–7). Write two sentences illustrating the difference between *laugh* and *laugh at*. (**1 SD 204a**)
4. *fail to see anything amusing* (l. 8). Explain the meaning of *amusing* here. Write sentences using the following words: *amuse, enjoy, entertain.* (**1 SD 168b**)
5. *A man had broken his right leg. He was taken to hospital a few weeks before Christmas.* (ll. 22–23.) Join these two sentences then compare your answer with the sentence in the passage. (**1 SD 78**)
6. *he kept on pestering his doctor* (l. 23). Write sentences using the following: *keep off, keep up with, keep out.* (**1 SD 196**)
7. *on New Year's Eve he was able to hobble along to a party* (ll. 30–31). Write two sentences using *could* and *was able to*. (**1 KS 107c**)

Multiple Choice Questions

a Choose the one answer (A, B, C or D) which you think is correct in the following:
How did the man break his left leg?

A By drinking more than was good for him;
B By not looking where he was going;
C By accidentally treading on some ice and falling;
D By slipping on the wet pavement.

b Choose the two answers which you think are correct in each of the following:
1. *On New Year's Eve the man felt ... and was able to go to a party.*

A miserable   B well   C recovery   D better   E dreadful

2. *When you have read the story you ... judge for yourself.*

A could   B will be able to   C were able to   D will manage to   E can

3. *The doctor let him go to the party ... he was well enough to leave hospital.*

A because   B until   C since   D as soon   E just

30 The Death of a Ghost

For years, villagers believed that Endley farm was haunted. The farm was owned by two brothers, Joe and Bert Cox. They employed a few farm hands, but no one
5 was willing to work there long. Every time a worker gave up his job, he told the same story. Farm labourers said that they always woke up to find that work had been done overnight. Hay had been cut
10 and cow sheds had been cleaned. A farm worker, who stayed up all night, claimed to have seen a figure cutting corn in the moonlight. In time, it became an accepted fact that the Cox brothers employed a
15 conscientious ghost that did most of their work for them.

the ghost of Endley

No one suspected that there might be someone else on the farm who had never been seen. This was indeed the case. A short time ago, villagers were astonished to learn that the ghost of Endley had died. Everyone went to the
20 funeral, for the 'ghost' was none other than Eric Cox, a third brother who was supposed to have died as a young man. After the funeral, Joe and Bert revealed a secret which they had kept for over forty years.

Eric had been the eldest son of the family. He had been obliged to join the army during the first World War. As he hated army life, he decided to desert his
25 regiment. When he learnt that he would be sent abroad, he returned to the farm and his father hid him until the end of the war. Fearing the authorities, Eric remained in hiding after the war as well. His father told everybody that Eric had been killed in action. The only other people who knew the secret were Joe and Bert. They did not even tell their wives. When their father died, they thought
30 it their duty to keep Eric in hiding. All these years, Eric had lived as a recluse. He used to sleep during the day and work at night, quite unaware of the fact that he had become the ghost of Endley. When he died, however, his brothers found it impossible to keep the secret any longer.

Comprehension

Give short answers to these questions in your own words as far as possible. Use one complete sentence for each answer.

a Why did farm hands frequently give up their jobs at Endley farm?
b Who was the ghost of Endley?
c Why was everybody surprised to learn that Eric Cox had just died?

Vocabulary

Explain the meanings of the following words and phrases as they are used in the passage: was willing (l. 5); labourers (l. 7); claimed (l. 11); an accepted fact (ll. 13–14); conscientious (l. 15); astonished (l. 19); revealed (l. 21).

Précis

In not more than 80 words write an account of the life of Eric Cox from the time he joined the army. Use your own words as far as possible. Do not include anything that is not in the last paragraph.

Composition

In not more than 250 words write an imaginary account of the night a farm worker saw a figure cutting corn. Write in the first person. Use the ideas given below. Do not write more than four paragraphs.
Title: The Ghost of Endley.
Introduction: I noticed that work had been done overnight. I decided to stay up all night—sat in barn.
Development: I fell asleep—suddenly woke up—went to cow-shed—it had already been cleaned—went out to fields—saw a figure working—rushed back to farmhouse—woke up others—we went out—no one there.
Conclusion: Sure it was a ghost—decided not to work at Endley farm any longer—told story to villagers.

Letter-writing

You have already written several letters to a friend but he has failed to answer them. Write a letter of about 100 words in three paragraphs complaining that he has not written to you and asking him to give news of himself.

Key Structures and Special Difficulties

Exercises

1. *Every time a worker gave up his job* . . . (ll. 5–6). Explain the meaning of the verb *gave up* here. Write sentences using the following: *give in, give away* and *give oneself up* (1 SD 48a)
2. *he told the same story* (ll. 6–7). Write sentences using *say* or *tell* with the following words: a lie, goodbye, the difference, so, the time. (1 SD 164)
3. *that did most of their work* (ll. 15–16). Write sentences using *do* or *make* with the following: a speech, his best, a favour, a mistake. (1 SD 102)
4. *The 'ghost' was none other than Eric Cox, a third brother who was supposed to have died as a young man.* (ll. 20–21.) Write three sentences using the following: I suppose; He is supposed; He was supposed. (SD 25)
5. *After the funeral, Joe and Bert revealed a secret. They had kept it for over forty years.* (ll. 21–22.) Join these two sentences then compare your answer with the sentence in the passage. (1 SD 78)
6. *He used to sleep during the day.* (ll. 30–31.) Write two sentences using: *He used to work* . . .; *He was working* . . . (1 KS 83)

Multiple Choice Questions

Choose the one answer (A, B, C or D) which you think is correct in the following:
No one learnt the secret about Eric because:

A his father had died;
B he lived alone;
C everyone believed he was a ghost;
D his brothers didn't tell anyone they were hiding him.

31   A Lovable Eccentric

True eccentrics never deliberately set out
to draw attention to themselves. They
disregard social conventions without being
conscious that they are doing anything
5 extraordinary. This invariably wins them
the love and respect of others, for they
add colour to the dull routine of everyday
life.

Up to the time of his death, Richard
10 Colson was one of the most notable
figures in our town. He was a shrewd and
wealthy business-man, but the ordinary
town-folk hardly knew anything about
this side of his life. He was known to us
15 all as Dickie and his eccentricity had
become legendary long before he died.

add colour to the dull routine

Dickie disliked snobs intensely. Though he owned a large car, he hardly ever
used it, preferring always to go on foot. Even when it was raining heavily, he
refused to carry an umbrella. One day, he walked into an expensive shop after
20 having been caught in a particularly heavy shower. He wanted to buy a £300
fur coat for his wife, but he was in such a bedraggled condition that an assistant
refused to serve him. Dickie left the shop without a word and returned carrying
a large cloth bag. As it was extremely heavy, he dumped it on the counter. The
assistant asked him to leave, but Dickie paid no attention to him and requested
25 to see the manager. Recognizing who the customer was, the manager was most
apologetic and reprimanded the assistant severely. When Dickie was given the
fur coat, he presented the assistant with the cloth bag. It contained £300 in
pennies. He insisted on the assistant's counting the money before he left—
72,000 pennies in all! On another occasion, he invited a number of important
30 critics to see his private collection of modern paintings. This exhibition received
a great deal of attention in the press, for though the pictures were supposed to
be the work of famous artists, they had in fact been painted by Dickie. It took
him four years to stage this elaborate joke simply to prove that critics do not
always know what they are talking about.

Comprehension

Give short answers to these questions in your own words as far as possible. Use one
complete sentence for each answer.
a Why do eccentrics add colour to the dull routine of everyday life?
b Why was Richard Colson one of the most notable figures of our town?
c What did Colson set out to prove when he held an exhibition of modern painting?

Vocabulary

Explain the meanings of the following words and phrases as they are used in the
passage: deliberately (l. 1); disregard (l. 3); conventions (l. 3); conscious (l. 4); notable
figures (ll. 10–11); shrewd (l. 11); elaborate (l. 33).

Précis

In not more than 80 words explain how Dickie bought a fur coat for his wife. Use your own words as far as possible. Do not include anything that is not in the last paragraph.

Composition

In not more than 250 words write an actual or imaginary description of an eccentric person. Expand the ideas given below into a plan and provide a suitable title. Your composition should be in three or four paragraphs.

Ideas: Appearance—dress—behaviour—home—way he or she lives—strange actions (e.g. puts up strange notices to passers-by in his garden; stands for parliament—gives speeches saying what he would do if he were Prime Minister—gets a few votes etc.) The way other people behave towards him.

Letter-writing

An old friend of yours has just died. Write a letter of about 100 words in three paragraphs to his wife expressing your sympathy and asking if you can help her in any way.

Key Structures and Special Difficulties

Exercises

1. *without being conscious* (ll. 3–4). Write sentences using verbs after each of the following: instead of; apart from; interested in. (**1 KS 51**)
2. *He owned a large car. He hardly ever used it. He preferred always to go on foot.* (ll. 17–18.) Join these three sentences then compare your answer with the sentence in the passage. (**1 KS 127**)
3. *he walked into an expensive shop* (l. 19). Write two pairs of sentences illustrating the difference between: *into* and *out of*; *into* and *in*. (**1 KS 87b**)
4. *Dickie paid no attention.* (l. 24.) Write sentences using the following: *pay attention, care* and *take care.* (**1 SD 44b**)
5. *Recognizing who the customer was.* (l. 25.) Write sentences completing the following: I don't know who . . .; Ask him why . . .; She asked if . . . (**1 KS 99**)
6. *He insisted on the assistant's counting the money.* (l. 28.) Complete the following: Would you mind my . . .; Fancy her . . . (**1 KS 166b**)
7. *72,000 pennies in all.* (l. 29.) Write sentences using the following phrases: *in the end*; *in debt*; *in sight*; *in tears*. (**SD 15**)

Multiple Choice Questions

a Choose the one answer (A, B, C or D) which you think is correct in the following:
When did Dickie leave the shop for the second time?

A   As soon as he bought the fur coat;
B   Not until the assistant had counted the pennies;
C   When he gave the assistant the cloth bag;
D   After the manager had scolded the assistant.

b Choose the two answers which you think are correct in each of the following:

1. *A lot of people came to the exhibition because they . . . the pictures were by famous artists.*

A knew   B thought   C hoped   D believed   E had been told

2. *He insisted . . . the money before he left.*

A that the assistant should count   B the assistant to count   C to count   D to be counted   E on the assistant's counting

32   A Lost Ship

The salvage operation had been a complete failure. The small ship, *Elkor*, which had been searching the Barents Sea for weeks, was on its way home. A radio message from the mainland had been received by the ship's captain instructing him to give up the search. The captain knew that another attempt would be made later, for the sunken ship he was trying to find had been carrying a precious cargo of gold bullion.

tremendous excitement on board

Despite the message, the captain of the *Elkor* decided to try once more. The seabed was scoured with powerful nets and there was tremendous excitement on board when a chest was raised from the bottom. Though the crew were at first under the impression that the lost ship had been found, the contents of the sea-chest proved them wrong. What they had in fact found was a ship which had been sunk many years before.

The chest contained the personal belongings of a seaman, Alan Fielding. There were books, clothing and photographs, together with letters which the seaman had once received from his wife. The captain of the *Elkor* ordered his men to salvage as much as possible from the wreck. Nothing of value was found, but the numerous items which were brought to the surface proved to be of great interest. From a heavy gun that was raised, the captain realized that the ship must have been a cruiser. In another sea-chest, which contained the belongings of a ship's officer, there was an unfinished letter which had been written on March 14th, 1943. The captain learnt from the letter that the name of the lost ship was the *Karen*. The most valuable find of all was the ship's log book, parts of which it was still possible to read. From this the captain was able to piece together all the information that had come to light. The *Karen* had been sailing in a convoy to Russia when she was torpedoed by an enemy submarine. This was later confirmed by a naval official at the Ministry of Defence after the *Elkor* had returned home. All the items that were found were sent to the War Museum.

Comprehension

a Why did the captain of *Elkor* know that another attempt would be made later to find the sunken ship?

b What did the crew think when a sea-chest was raised from the bottom?

c Who was Alan Fielding?

Vocabulary

Explain the meanings of the following words and phrases as they are used in the passage: instructing (ll. 6–7); give up the search (l. 7); precious (l. 11); tremendous (l. 15); were at first under the impression (l. 17); wrong (l. 18).

Précis

In not more than 80 words describe how the items brought to the surface enabled the captain of *Elkor* to identify the lost ship. Use your own words as far as possible. Do not include anything that is not in the last paragraph.

Composition

In not more than 250 words write the page of *Karen's* log book which was dated March 14th, 1943. Use the ideas given below. Do not write more than four paragraphs.
Title: The Last Day.
Introduction: Journey has gone well so far—convoy successfully fought off an air attack—early morning—no ships lost.
Development and Conclusion: 10 a.m. First attack by U-boat—ship ahead, the *Dauntless* sunk—men in sea—*Karen* picked up survivors—720 men—50 lives lost—crowded on board—attack on U-boat—puts it out of action with depth charges. 3.15 p.m. (last entry)—second U-boat attack . . .

Letter-writing

In about 100 words write the unfinished letter referred to in the passage which was written on March 14th, 1943 by a ship's officer.

Key Structures and Special Difficulties

Exercises

1. *which had been searching the Barents Sea* (ll. 3–4). Write sentences using the following: *had been doing* and *had been working.* (1 KS 153b)
2. *received* (l. 6). Write two sentences illustrating the difference between *receive* and *take.* (1 SD 20)
3. *The sea-bed was scoured with powerful nets. There was tremendous excitement on board. A chest was raised from the bottom. The crew were at first under the impression that the lost ship had been found. The contents of the sea-chest proved them wrong.* (ll. 13–18.) Express these ideas again in not more than two sentences. Compare your answer with the sentences in the passage. (1 KS 71 and 127)
4. *the contents of the sea-chest* (l. 18). How would the word *contents* be stressed in this sentence? (1 SD 226)
5. *clothing* (l. 21). Write three sentences using the following words: *cloth, clothes,* and *clothing.* (1 SD 202a)
6. *brought* (l. 24). Write three sentences using the following words: *bring, take,* and *fetch.* (1 SD 80b)
7. *realized* (l. 25). Write two sentences illustrating the difference between *realize* and *understand.* (1 SD 52c)

Multiple Choice Questions

a Choose the one answer (A, B, C or D) which you think is correct in the following:
The Karen *failed to reach Russia:*

A   so she returned home;
B   although she was travelling in convoy;
C   because there was a war;
D   because she was sunk by a submarine.

b Choose the two answers which you think are correct in the following:
When he saw the heavy gun the captain knew the lost ship . . . a cruiser.

A had to be   B must have been   C should have been   D ought to be   E had been

33   A Day to Remember

We have all experienced days when everything goes wrong. A day may begin well enough, but suddenly everything seems to get out of control. What invariably happens is that a great number of things choose to go wrong at precisely the same moment. It is as if a single unimportant event set up a chain of reactions. Let us suppose that you are preparing a meal and keeping an eye on the baby at the same time. The telephone rings and this marks the prelude to an unforeseen series of catastrophes. While you are on the phone, the baby pulls the table-cloth off the table, smashing half your best crockery and cutting himself in the process. You

just one of those days!

hang up hurriedly and attend to baby, crockery, etc. Meanwhile, the meal gets burnt. As if this were not enough to reduce you to tears, your husband arrives, unexpectedly bringing three guests to dinner.

Things can go wrong on a big scale as a number of people recently discovered in Parramatta, a suburb of Sydney. During the rush hour one evening two cars collided and both drivers began to argue. The woman immediately behind the two cars happened to be a learner. She suddenly got into a panic and stopped her car. This made the driver following her brake hard. His wife was sitting beside him holding a large cake. As she was thrown forward, the cake went right through the windscreen and landed on the road. Seeing a cake flying through the air, a lorry-driver who was drawing up alongside the car, pulled up all of a sudden. The lorry was loaded with empty beer bottles and hundreds of them slid off the back of the vehicle and on to the road. This led to yet another angry argument. Meanwhile, the traffic piled up behind. It took the police nearly an hour to get the traffic on the move again. In the meantime, the lorry-driver had to sweep up hundreds of broken bottles. Only two stray dogs benefited from all this confusion, for they greedily devoured what was left of the cake. It was just one of those days!

Comprehension

Give short answers to these questions in your own words as far as possible. Use one complete sentence for each answer.
a What can mark the beginning of an unforeseen series of catastrophes while you are preparing a meal?
b Why are your husband's guests not welcome?
c What began all the trouble in Parramatta recently?

Vocabulary

Explain the meanings of the following words and phrases as they are used in the passage: happens (l. 5); precisely (l. 6); preparing (l. 9); catastrophes (l. 13); smashing (l. 15); in the process (l. 16); reduce you to tears (l. 18).

Précis

In not more than 80 words describe what happened from the time when the learner driver stopped her car. Use your own words as far as possible. Do not include anything that is not in the last paragraph.

Composition

In not more than 250 words describe a similar 'chain of reactions'. Expand the ideas given below into a plan and provide a suitable title. Your composition should be in three or four paragraphs.

Ideas: Man loaded with parcels—looking for his car—saw one exactly like it—mistook it for his own—found his key with difficulty—tried to open the door—key wouldn't turn—forced the lock—broke the key—dropped the parcels—infuriated—deliberately broke the window of the car—the owner saw him—rushed towards him—called a policeman—the man arrested—tried to explain—was not believed.

Letter-writing

You have been trying to sell your car and an unknown person has written to you making an offer. Write a reply in about 100 words in three paragraphs accepting the offer and making arrangements for the sale.

Key Structures and Special Difficulties

Exercises

1. *We have all experienced days* . . . (l. 1). Write two sentences using the following: *he experienced; a lot of experience.* (**1 SD 84a**)
2. *A day may begin well enough* (ll. 2–3). Write sentences using the following: *good enough; enough money; fairly.* (**1 SD 212a**)
3. *You are on the phone. The baby pulls the table-cloth off the table. He smashes half your best crockery. He cuts himself in the process.* (ll. 13–16.) Join these sentences together to make one sentence. Compare your answer with the sentence in the passage. (**1 KS 127**)
4. *people recently discovered* (l. 20). Write two sentences illustrating the difference between *discover* and *invent.* (**1 SD 152a**)
5. *His wife was sitting beside him.* (ll. 24–25.) Write two sentences illustrating the difference between *beside* and *besides.* (**1 SD 48b**)
6. *a lorry-driver who was drawing up alongside the car* (l. 27). Explain the meaning of *drawing up* in this sentence. Write sentences using *draw back* and *draw off.* (**1 SD 158**)
7. *the lorry-driver had to sweep up hundreds of broken bottles* (ll. 31–32). Write two sentences illustrating the difference between *had to take* and *should have taken.* (**1 KS 160b**)

Multiple Choice Questions

a Choose the one answer (A, B, C or D) which you think is correct in the following:
The lorry stopped suddenly:

A   in order not to hit the car in front;
B   in order to draw up alongside the car;
C   because the driver didn't want to run over the dogs;
D   because the driver had seen a cake in the air.

b Choose the two answers which you think are correct in the following:
An unforeseen series of catastrophes . . . the traffic jam.

A led to   B caused   C found   D came from   E did

34   A Happy Discovery

Antique shops exert a peculiar fascination
on a great many people. The more expensive kind of antique shop where rare
objects are beautifully displayed in glass
5 cases to keep them free from dust is
usually a forbidding place. But no one has
to muster up courage to enter a less
pretentious antique shop. There is always
hope that in its labyrinth of musty, dark,
10 disordered rooms a real rarity will be
found amongst the piles of assorted junk
that litter the floors.

*No one discovers a rarity
by chance*

   No one discovers a rarity by chance. A
truly dedicated searcher for art treasures
15 must have patience, and above all, the
ability to recognize the worth of some-
thing when he sees it. To do this, he must be at least as knowledgeable as the
dealer. Like a scientist bent on making a discovery, he must cherish the hope that
one day he will be amply rewarded.
20   My old friend, Frank Halliday, is just such a person. He has often described
to me how he picked up a masterpiece for a mere £5. One Saturday morning,
Frank visited an antique shop in my neighbourhood. As he had never been there
before, he found a great deal to interest him. The morning passed rapidly and
Frank was about to leave when he noticed a large packing-case lying on the floor.
25 The dealer told him that it had just come in, but that he could not be bothered
to open it. Frank begged him to do so and the dealer reluctantly prised it open.
The contents were disappointing. Apart from an interesting-looking carved
dagger, the box was full of crockery, much of it broken. Frank gently lifted the
crockery out of the box and suddenly noticed a miniature painting at the bottom
30 of the packing-case. As its composition and line reminded him of an Italian
painting he knew well, he decided to buy it. Glancing at it briefly, the dealer
told him that it was worth £5. Frank could hardly conceal his excitement, for
he knew that he had made a real discovery. The tiny painting proved to be an
unknown masterpiece by Correggio and was worth thousands of pounds.

Comprehension

Give short answers to these questions in your own words as far as possible. Use one
complete sentence for each answer.
a What does a truly dedicated searcher hope to find in the less pretentious kind of
antique shop?
b What qualities must a truly dedicated searcher possess?
c How much did Frank Halliday pay for his masterpiece?

Vocabulary

Explain the meanings of the following words and phrases as they are used in the
passage: rare objects (ll. 3–4); displayed (l. 4); piles (l. 11); assorted junk (l. 11); truly
(l. 14); bent on (l. 18); amply (l. 19).

Précis

In not more than 80 words describe how Frank Halliday came to discover an unknown masterpiece. Use your own words as far as possible. Do not include anything that is not in the last paragraph.

Composition

In not more than 250 words write a description, real or imaginary, of an antique shop. Use the ideas given below. Do not write more than four paragraphs.
Title: An Antique Shop.
Introduction: Appearance outside—window display—the sort of people it attracts.
Development: Inside—the dealer—his appearance and character—the shop itself—how objects are displayed—a typical scene during the day—description of customers.
Conclusion: The pleasure of searching for unusual things.

Letter-writing

You intend to spend your holidays in a country which has a very warm (or very cold) climate. Write a letter of about 100 words in three paragraphs to a friend asking him to advise you about items of clothing you should take with you.

Key Structures and Special Difficulties

Exercises
1. *when he sees it* (l. 17). Write sentences using the following: *the moment he arrives*; *until he comes*; and *before you leave*. (**1 KS 150c**)
2. Explain the difference in the use of *must be* in these two sentences:
   To do this, he *must be* at least as knowledgeable as the dealer. (l. 17.)
   You *must be* very tired after driving so many miles. (**1 KS 45**)
3. Supply *a(n)* or *the* where necessary in the following. Do not refer to the passage until you finish the exercise:
   One Saturday morning, ... Frank visited ... antique shop in my neighbourhood. As he had never been there before, he found ... great deal to interest him. ... morning passed rapidly and ... Frank was about to leave when he noticed ... large packing-case lying on ... floor. ... dealer told him that it had just come in, but that he could not be bothered to open it. ... Frank begged him to do so and ... dealer reluctantly prised it open. ... contents were disappointing. Apart from ... interesting-looking carved dagger, ... box was full of ... crockery, much of it broken. (ll. 21–28.) (**1 KS 23, 81, 138**)
4. *he noticed* (l. 24). Write two sentences illustrating the difference between *notice* and *remark*. (**1 SD 104**)

Multiple Choice Questions

a Choose the one answer (A, B, C or D) which you think is correct in the following:
Frank decided to buy the miniature because:

A it was an Italian painting he knew well;
B it only cost £5;
C he knew he had made a real discovery;
D it was similar to a painting he knew well.

b Choose the two answers which you think are correct in the following:
... an interesting-looking dagger, there wasn't anything in the box.

A Except   B Only   C Apart from   D Unless   E Except for

35 Justice Was Done

The word *justice* is usually associated with courts of law. We might say that justice has been done when a man's innocence or guilt has been proved beyond doubt.
5 Justice is part of the complex machinery of the law. Those who seek it, undertake an arduous journey and can never be sure that they will find it. Judges, however wise or eminent, are human and can make
10 mistakes.

There are rare instances when justice almost ceases to be an abstract conception. Reward or punishment are meted out quite independent of human inter-
15 ference. At such times, justice acts like a living force. When we use a phrase like

the cry was repeated several times

'it serves him right', we are, in part, admitting that a certain set of circumstances has enabled justice to act of its own accord.

When a thief was caught on the premises of a large fur store one morning, the
20 shop assistants must have found it impossible to resist the temptation to say 'it serves him right'. The shop was an old-fashioned one with many large, disused fireplaces and tall, narrow chimneys. Towards midday, a girl heard a muffled cry coming from behind one of the walls. As the cry was repeated several times, she ran to tell the manager who promptly rang up the fire-brigade. The cry had
25 certainly come from one of the chimneys, but as there were so many of them, the firemen could not be certain which one it was. They located the right chimney by tapping at the walls and listening for the man's cries. After chipping through a wall which was eighteen inches thick, they found that a man had been trapped in the chimney. As it was extremely narrow, the man was unable to
30 move, but the firemen were eventually able to free him by cutting a huge hole in the wall. The sorry-looking, blackened figure that emerged, at once admitted that he had tried to break into the shop during the night but had got stuck in the chimney. He had been there for nearly ten hours. Justice had been done even before the man was handed over to the police.

Comprehension

Give short answers to these questions in your own words as far as possible. Use one complete sentence for each answer.
a What is the word *justice* usually associated with?
b Why can those who seek justice never be sure that they will find it?
c When does justice seem to act like a living force?

Vocabulary

Explain the meanings of the following words and phrases as they are used in the passage: seek (l. 6); arduous (l. 7); eminent (l. 9); instances (l. 11); ceases (l. 12); independent of (l. 14); of its own accord (l. 18).

Précis

In not more than 80 words describe how the thief came to be discovered up the chimney and how he was freed. Use your own words as far as possible. Do not include anything that is not in the last paragraph.

Composition

In not more than 250 words write an imaginary account of the thief's experiences up to the time he was freed by firemen. Expand the ideas given below into a plan and provide a suitable title. Your composition should be in three or four paragraphs.

Ideas: Planning the theft—kept close watch on shop—noticed chimneys—one night climbed on to roof—chimney seemed wide—went down—stuck—climbed up again—went down another chimney—again got stuck—could neither climb up nor down—shouted for help—everything dark and silent—frightened—shouted next morning—freed by firemen.

Letter-writing

You recently quarrelled with a friend. Write him a letter of about 100 words in three paragraphs apologizing for the incident and suggesting that you should both meet soon.

Key Structures and Special Difficulties

Exercises

1. *We might say that justice has been done . . .* (ll. 2–3).
   Complete the following sentences: (**1 KS 41**)
   He says that . . .
   He wants to know if . . .
   He believes that . . .
2. *when a man's innocence or guilt has been proved beyond doubt* (ll. 3–4). Write sentences using the following: *The moment he has arrived . . .; Now that you have finished . . .* (**1 KS 151c**)
3. *They chipped through a wall. It was eighteen inches thick. They found a man. He had been trapped in the chimney.* (ll. 27–29.) Join these sentences together to make a single sentence. Compare your answer with the sentence in the passage. (**1 KS 127**)
4. *they found that a man had been trapped in the chimney* (ll. 28–29). What is the plural of the following words: chimney, valley, baby, day, hobby, army, money, victory, turkey and storey. (**SD 47**)
5. Give the correct form of the verbs in brackets. Do not refer to the passage until you finish the exercise:
   The sorry-looking, blackened figure that emerged, at once (admit) that he (try) to break into the shop during the night but (get) stuck in the chimney. He (be) there for nearly ten hours. Justice (do) even before the man was handed over to the police. (ll. 31–34.) (**1 KS 97**)

Multiple Choice Questions

Choose the two answers which you think are correct in each of the following:

1. *As the chimney was extremely narrow, it was impossible . . . move.*

   A for to   B to   C for him to   D for   E in order to

2. *The sorry-looking figure at once . . . that he had tried to break in.*

   A denied   B confessed   C refused   D said   E told

36   A Chance in a Million

We are less credulous than we used to be.
In the nineteenth century, a novelist
would bring his story to a conclusion by
presenting his readers with a series of
5 coincidences—most of them wildly improbable. Readers happily accepted the
fact that an obscure maid-servant was
really the hero's mother. A long-lost
brother, who was presumed dead, was
10 really alive all the time and wickedly
plotting to bring about the hero's down-
fall. And so on. Modern readers would
find such naive solutions totally unaccept-
able. Yet, in real life, circumstances do
15 sometimes conspire to bring about coincidences which anyone but a nineteenth
century novelist would find incredible.

recently found a brother

A German taxi-driver, Franz Bussman, recently found a brother who was
thought to have been killed twenty years before. While on a walking tour with
20 his wife, he stopped to talk to a workman. After they had gone on, Mrs Bussman
commented on the workman's close resemblance to her husband and even
suggested that he might be his brother. Franz poured scorn on the idea, pointing
out that his brother had been killed in action during the war. Though Mrs
Bussman was fully acquainted with this story, she thought that there was a
25 chance in a million that she might be right. A few days later, she sent a boy to
the workman to ask him if his name was Hans Bussman. Needless to say, the
man's name was Hans Bussman and he really was Franz's long-lost brother.
When the brothers were re-united, Hans explained how it was that he was still
alive. After having been wounded towards the end of the war, he had been sent
30 to hospital and was separated from his unit. The hospital had been bombed and
Hans had made his way back into Western Germany on foot. Meanwhile, his
unit was lost and all records of him had been destroyed. Hans returned to his
family home, but the house had been bombed and no one in the neighbourhood
knew what had become of the inhabitants. Assuming that his family had been
35 killed during an air-raid, Hans settled down in a village fifty miles away where
he had remained ever since.

Comprehension

Give short answers to these questions in your own words as far as possible. Use one
complete sentence for each answer.
a How did many nineteenth century novels end?
b Why was Mrs Bussman struck by the workman's appearance?
c How did Mrs Bussman find out the identity of the workman?

Vocabulary

Explain the meanings of the following words and phrases as they are used in the
passage: credulous (l. 1); a conclusion (l. 3); improbable (ll. 5–6); presumed (l. 9);
plotting (l. 11); totally (l. 13); bring about (l. 15).

Précis

In not more than 80 words write an account of what happened to Hans Bussman from the time he was wounded to the time he was re-united with his brother. Use your own words as far as possible. Do not include anything that is not in the last paragraph.

Composition

In not more than 250 words write an imaginary account of Franz Bussman's life story up to the time he was re-united with his brother. Use the ideas given below. Do not write more than four paragraphs.

Title: The Past.

Introduction: Tried to get information about Hans—none available—gave up search.

Development: Found it hard to settle down—moved from place to place and from job to job—how he met Mrs Bussman—marriage—settled down at last—became a cook—disliked the work—went into partnership with a friend—became a taxi-driver—once visited home town—block of flats where his house used to be—no one remembered him.

Conclusion: Future plans now that Hans has been found.

Letter-writing

Write a letter of about 100 words in three paragraphs to your employer informing him that you will be absent from work for a few days because you are ill. Point out anything important that should be attended to in your absence and say when you hope to be back.

Key Structures and Special Difficulties

Exercises

1. *We are less credulous than we used to be. In the nineteenth century, a novelist would bring his story* . . . (ll. 1–3). Supply *used to* and *would* in the following:
When I was young I . . . have a lot more free time than I do now. I . . . live near my work and . . . always get home early. Sometimes I . . . do a bit of gardening or go for a long walk. (1 KS 139b)
2. *Readers happily accepted the fact.* (ll. 6–7.) Write two sentences illustrating the difference between *accept* and *agree.* (1 SD 160b)
3. *the hero's mother* (l. 8). Supply apostrophes in the following: Georges umbrella; that womans handbag; Keats poetry; the childrens clothes; the soldiers uniforms; in six hours time; a hundred pounds worth (1 SD 38)
4. *After having been wounded.* (l. 29.) Write two sentences beginning with *After having been . . .* (1 KS 167)
5. *he had been sent to hospital* (ll. 29–30). Write sentences using the following words: *school, market, cinema.* (1 KS 138c)

Multiple Choice Questions

Choose the one answer (A, B, C or D) which you think is correct in the following:

Why had Hans settled down in a village fifty miles away from the place where his family had lived?

A Because he wanted to be near home;
B Because he hoped he would find his brother;
C Because he believed that no one in his family was still alive;
D Because he didn't want to be reminded of the tragedy.

37 The Westhaven Express

We have learnt to expect that trains will
be punctual. After years of pre-con-
ditioning, most of us have developed an
unshakable faith in railway time-tables.
5 Ships may be delayed by storms; air
flights may be cancelled because of bad
weather; but trains must be on time. Only
an exceptionally heavy snow fall might
temporarily dislocate railway services. It
10 is all too easy to blame the railway
authorities when something does go
wrong. The truth is that when mistakes
occur, they are more likely to be *ours* than
theirs.

*an unshakable faith in
time-tables*

15   After consulting my railway time-table,
I noted with satisfaction that there was an
express train to Westhaven. It went direct from my local station and the journey
lasted a mere hour and seventeen minutes. When I boarded the train, I could not
help noticing that a great many local people got on as well. At the time, this did
20 not strike me as odd. I reflected that there must be a great many people besides
myself who wished to take advantage of this excellent service. Neither was I
surprised when the train stopped at Widley, a tiny station a few miles along the
line. Even a mighty express train can be held up by signals. But when the train
dawdled at station after station, I began to wonder. It suddenly dawned on me
25 that this express was not roaring down the line at ninety miles an hour, but
barely chugging along at thirty. One hour and seventeen minutes passed and we
had not even covered half the distance. I asked a passenger if this was the
Westhaven Express, but he had not even heard of it. I determined to lodge a
complaint as soon as we arrived. Two hours later, I was talking angrily to the
30 station-master at Westhaven. When he denied the train's existence, I borrowed
his copy of the time-table. There was a note of triumph in my voice when I told
him that it was there in black and white. Glancing at it briefly, he told me to
look again. A tiny asterisk conducted me to a footnote at the bottom of the page.
It said: 'This service has been suspended.'

Comprehension

Give short answers to these questions in your own words as far as possible. Use one
complete sentence for each answer.
a Why have we developed an unshakable faith in railway time-tables?
b How long was the journey from the writer's village to Westhaven supposed to take
by express train?
c How did the writer explain the fact that many local people boarded the train at the
same time as he did?

Vocabulary

Explain the meanings of the following words and phrases as they are used in the
passage: punctual (l. 2); unshakable faith (l. 4); delayed (l. 5); cancelled (l. 6); temporarily dislocate (l. 9); consulting (l. 15); a mere (l. 18)

Précis

In not more than 80 words, write an account of the writer's experiences from the moment he boarded the train. Use your own words as far as possible. Do not include anything that is not in the last paragraph.

Composition

In not more than 250 words describe a journey by train. Though you wished to take a slow train, you accidentally got on a fast one. Expand the ideas given below into a plan and provide a suitable title. Your composition should not be more than four paragraphs.

Ideas: Got on train—expected it to stop—prepared to alight—it went straight on—very fast—you asked passengers—learnt it was an express—ticket collector came along—you explained situation—had to pay full fare—journey lasted two hours—arrived miles away from destination—no fast train back—had to board a slow one!

Letter-Writing

A young couple you know have just had their first child: a baby girl. Write a letter of about 100 words in three paragraphs congratulating them. Inquire about the health of mother and child and say that you hope to be able to visit them soon.

Key Structures and Special Difficulties

Exercises

1. *It is all too easy to blame the railway authorities.* (ll. 9–11.) Note this pattern. Join the following sentences using the words in brackets: (1 SD 210)
   The wall is high. I cannot climb it. (too)
   The wall is low. I can climb it. (enough)
2. *I could not help noticing.* (ll. 18–19.) Complete the following sentences. (1 KS 166)
   I can't stand . . .
   I don't mind . . .
3. *Neither was I surprised . . .* (ll. 21–22). Write sentences beginning with the following words: *Never . . .*; *Hardly . . .*; *Little . . .* (SD 21)
4. *seventeen minutes passed* (l. 26). Write two sentences illustrating the difference between *passed* and *past*. (1 SD 88a)
5. *he denied the train's existence* (l. 30). Write two sentences illustrating the difference between *refuse* and *deny*. (1 SD 80a)
6. *I borrowed his copy of the time-table.* (ll. 30–31.) Write two sentences illustrating the difference between *borrow* and *lend*. (1 SD 34c)

Multiple Choice Questions

a Choose the one answer (A, B, C or D) which you think is correct in the following:
The author learnt that the Westhaven Express did not exist:

A from a passenger on the train;
B from the station-master at Westhaven;
C from an old time-table he had at home;
D from a footnote in the time-table he borrowed from the station-master.

b Choose the two answers which you think are correct in the following:
. . . at it briefly, he told me to look again.

A Looking B He looked C After looking D Looked E From looking

93

38   The First Calendar

Future historians will be in a unique position when they come to record the history of our own times. They will hardly know which facts to select from
5 the great mass of evidence that steadily accumulates. What is more, they will not have to rely solely on the written word. Films, gramophone records, and magnetic tapes will provide them with a bewilder-
10 ing amount of information. They will be able, as it were, to see and hear us in action. But the historian attempting to reconstruct the distant past is always faced with a difficult task. He has to
15 deduce what he can from the few scanty clues available. Even seemingly insignifi-
cant remains can shed interesting light on the history of early man.

*Future historians will be in a
unique position*

Up to now, historians have assumed that calendars came into being with the advent of agriculture, for then man was faced with a real need to understand
20 something about the seasons. Recent scientific evidence seems to indicate that this assumption is incorrect.

Historians have long been puzzled by dots, lines and symbols which have been engraved on walls, bones, and the ivory tusks of mammoths. The nomads who made these markings lived by hunting and fishing during the last Ice Age
25 which began about 35,000 B.C. and ended about 10,000 B.C. By correlating markings made in various parts of the world, historians have been able to read this difficult code. They have found that it is connected with the passage of days and the phases of the moon. It is, in fact, a primitive type of calendar. It has long been known that the hunting scenes depicted on walls were not simply
30 a form of artistic expression. They had a definite meaning, for they were as near as early man could get to writing. It is possible that there is a definite relation between these paintings and the markings that sometimes accompany them. It seems that man was making a real effort to understand the seasons 20,000 years earlier than has been supposed.

Comprehension

Give short answers to these questions in your own words as far as possible. Use one complete sentence for each answer.
a Why will future historians not have to rely entirely on the written word when they come to record the history of our own times?
b Why do historians who write about the distant past have a difficult task?
c When was it believed that calendars were first used?

Vocabulary

Explain the meanings of the following words and phrases as they are used in the passage: record (l. 2); select (l. 4); great mass of evidence (l. 5); accumulates (l. 6); solely (l. 7); bewildering (ll. 9–10); insignificant (ll. 16–17).

Precis

In not more than 80 words describe what historians have learnt from the strange markings made by early man. Use your own words as far as possible. Do not include anything that is not in the last paragraph.

Composition

In not more than 250 words describe some of the things future historians will be able to learn about us. Use the ideas given below. Do not write more than four paragraphs.
Title: Studying the Past.
Introduction: The future historian's sources: newspapers, magazines, books, films, recorded sound, existing buildings.
Development: Social and political history: how we dressed—what we ate—what houses we lived in—what our cities were like—the forms of entertainment we enjoyed —the news day by day—the way we fought our wars—great moments in history— leading figures of the time as well as ordinary people.
Conclusion: Study of history will provide interest and excitement—the past will be brought to life.

Letter-writing

For several years you have been writing to a pen-friend whom you have never met in person. Write him a letter of about 100 words in three paragraphs telling him that you will be visiting his country soon and expressing pleasure at the thought that you will be able to meet each other for the first time.

Key Structures and Special Difficulties

Exercises
1. Give the correct form of the verbs in brackets. Do not refer to the passage until you finish the exercise:
   Up to now, historians (assume) that calendars (come) into being with the advent of agriculture, for then man (face) with a real need to understand something about the seasons. Recent scientific evidence (seem) to indicate that this assumption (be) incorrect. Historians long (puzzle) by dots, lines and symbols which (engrave) on walls, bones, and the ivory tusks of mammoths. The nomads who (make) these markings (live) by hunting and fishing during the last Ice Age which (begin) about 35,000 B.C. and (end) about 10,000 B.C. (ll. 18–25.) (Mainly **1 KS 80**)
2. *it is connected with* (l. 27). Put *with* or *for* after the following verbs: agree, account, mistake, cope, correspond, apologize, blame, reason, satisfied, quarrel, wait, search. (**1 KS 114**)
3. *between these paintings and the markings* (l. 32). Write two sentences illustrating the difference between *between* and *among*. (**1 SD 192b**)

Multiple Choice Questions

Choose the two answers which you think are correct in each of the following:
1. *Early men drew pictures . . . they still hadn't learnt to write.*

   A though   B for   C because   D even if   E of which

2. *The people who lived by hunting and fishing during the last Ice Age . . .*

   A wandered from place to place   B lived in villages   C first learnt to write D were nomads   E learnt how to farm the land

39   Nothing to Worry About

The rough road across the plain soon became so bad that we tried to get Bruce to drive back to the village we had come from. Even though the road was littered
5 with boulders and pitted with holes, Bruce was not in the least perturbed. Glancing at his map, he informed us that the next village was a mere twenty miles away. It was not that Bruce always under-
10 estimated difficulties. He simply had no sense of danger at all. No matter what the conditions were, he believed that a car should be driven as fast as it could possibly go.

Bruce was not in the least perturbed

15   As we bumped over the dusty track, we swerved to avoid large boulders. The wheels scooped up stones which hammered ominously under the car. We felt sure that sooner or later a stone would rip a hole in our petrol tank or damage the engine. Because of this, we kept looking back, wondering if we were leaving a
20 trail of oil and petrol behind us.

What a relief it was when the boulders suddenly disappeared, giving way to a stretch of plain where the only obstacles were clumps of bushes. But there was worse to come. Just ahead of us there was a huge fissure. In response to renewed pleadings, Bruce stopped. Though we all got out to examine the fissure, he
25 remained in the car. We informed him that the fissure extended for fifty yards and was two feet wide and four feet deep. Even this had no effect. Bruce engaged low gear and drove at a terrifying speed, keeping the front wheels astride the crack as he followed its zig-zag course. Before we had time to worry about what might happen, we were back on the plain again. Bruce consulted the map once
30 more and told us that the village was now only fifteen miles away. Our next obstacle was a shallow pool of water about half a mile across. Bruce charged at it, but in the middle, the car came to a grinding halt. A yellow light on the dashboard flashed angrily and Bruce cheerfully announced that there was no oil in the engine!

Comprehension

Give short answers to these questions in your own words as far as possible. Use one complete sentence for each answer.

a Why did the passengers try to get Bruce to drive back to the village they had come from?

b Why was Bruce not perturbed by the bad state of the road?

c Why did the passengers keep looking back as Bruce swerved to avoid boulders?

Vocabulary

Explain the meanings of the following words and phrases as they are used in the passage: boulders (l. 5); perturbed (l. 6); under-estimated (ll. 9–10); bumped (l. 15); swerved (l. 16); hammered (l. 17); ominously (l. 17).

Précis

In not more than 80 words describe what happened from the time when the car got past the boulders to the moment it stopped in the shallow pool. Use your own words as far as possible. Do not include anything that is not in the last paragraph.

Composition

In not more than 250 words write a continuation to the passage. Expand the ideas given below into a plan and provide a suitable title. Your composition should be in four paragraphs.
Ideas: Got out—tried to push car—impossible—walked to next village—tried to get a taxi—no driver would take us over rough road—paid a large sum of money to rent a jeep—pulled car out of water—found engine badly damaged—Bruce undismayed.

Letter-writing

You are on holiday and are running out of money. Write an urgent letter to your father in about 100 words in three paragraphs, asking him to help you out of your difficulties.

Key Structures and Special Difficulties

Exercises
1. *we tried to get Bruce to drive back to the village* (ll. 2–3). Write these sentences again using *got* in place of *made*. (1 SD 162)
   I made him tell me the truth.
   He made me translate the article into English.
2. *he believed that a car should be driven* (ll. 12–13). Write two sentences beginning: *He suggested that . . .; He insisted that . . .* (1 KS 155)
3. *wondering if we were leaving* (l. 19). Complete the following sentences: (1 KS 155 Exercise D)
   Can he wait a few minutes longer? I wonder if . . .
   When will he arrive? I wonder when . . .
4. *we were leaving a trail of oil and petrol* (ll. 19–20). Write two sentences illustrating the difference between *petrol* and *benzine*. (1 SD 212b)
5. *What a relief it was . . .* (l. 21). Write these sentences again beginning each one with *What*: (1 SD 16)
   This is a wonderful garden!
   It is a terrible day!
6. *we all got out* (l. 24). Write sentences using the following: *get on*; *get over*; and *get through*. (1 SD 188a)
7. *Bruce . . . told us.* (ll. 29–30.) Write two sentences illustrating the difference between *say* and *tell*. (1 KS 41)

Multiple Choice Questions

Choose the one answer (A, B, C or D) which you think is correct in the following:
Bruce steered a zig-zag course:

A   in order the wheels wouldn't go into the fissure;
B   in order to keep the wheels out of the fissure;
C   in order that the wheels are out of the fissure;
D   in order to prevent the wheels from the fissure.

40 Who's Who

It has never been explained why university students seem to enjoy practical jokes more than anyone else. Students specialize in a particular type of practical joke: the hoax. Inviting the fire-brigade to put out a non-existent fire is a crude form of deception which no self-respecting student would ever indulge in. Students often create amusing situations which are funny to everyone except the victims.

The police attempted to seize the drill

When a student recently saw two workmen using a pneumatic drill outside his university, he immediately telephoned the police and informed them that two students dressed up as workmen were tearing up the road with a pneumatic drill. As soon as he had hung up, he went over to the workmen and told them that if a policeman ordered them to go away, they were not to take him seriously. He added that a student had dressed up as a policeman and was playing all sorts of silly jokes on people. Both the police and the workmen were grateful to the student for this piece of advance information.

The student hid in an archway nearby where he could watch and hear everything that went on. Sure enough, a policeman arrived on the scene and politely asked the workmen to go away. When he received a very rude reply from one of the workmen, he threatened to remove them by force. The workmen told him to do as he pleased and the policeman telephoned for help. Shortly afterwards, four more policemen arrived and remonstrated with the workmen. As the men refused to stop working, the police attempted to seize the pneumatic drill. The workmen struggled fiercely and one of them lost his temper. He threatened to call the police. At this, the police pointed out ironically that this would hardly be necessary as the men were already under arrest. Pretending to speak seriously, one of the workmen asked if he might make a telephone call before being taken to the station. Permission was granted and a policeman accompanied him to a call-box. Only when he saw that the man was actually telephoning the police did he realize that they had all been the victims of a hoax.

Comprehension

Give short answers to these questions in your own words as far as possible. Use one complete sentence for each answer.

a What sort of practical joke do students specialize in?
b What did the student tell the police?
c What did the student tell the workmen?

Vocabulary

Explain the meanings of the following words and phrases as they are used in the passage: a particular type (l. 4); put out (ll. 5–6); deception (l. 7); victims (l. 10); hung up (l. 17); silly (l. 20); grateful (l. 20).

Précis

In not more than 80 words describe what happened after the student hid in an archway. Use your own words as far as possible. Do not include anything that is not in the last paragraph.

Composition

Imagine that the policeman who accompanied the workman to the call-box did not realize that they had all been victims of a practical joke. In not more than 250 words, describe what happened. Use the ideas given below. Do not write more than four paragraphs.

Title: Arrest the Police!

Introduction: Policeman and worker returned—the other workman still quarrelling with police—resisting arrest.

Development: More police arrived—workmen told them that the first lot of policemen were students—the second lot of police threatened to arrest the first lot—asked for identity cards—the first lot said that the workmen were students—workers had to prove their identity.

Conclusion: Realized they were victims of a hoax.

Letter-writing

A friend has written to you offering you a place in his car on a long trip he intends to make, providing that you are willing to share expenses. In not more than 100 words, write a letter accepting his offer. Do not write more than three paragraphs.

Key Structures and Special Difficulties

Exercises

1. *to put out a non-existent fire* (ll. 5–6). Write sentences using the following: (1 **SD 76**) *put up, put someone up, put up with* and *put off.*
2. *funny to everyone except the victims* (l. 10). Write three sentences illustrating the use of the following: (1 **SD 40b**) *except, except for* and *apart from.*
3. *dressed up* (l. 15). Write two sentences illustrating the difference between *dress* and *dress up.* (1 **SD 160c**)
4. *he could watch* (l. 22). Write two sentences illustrating the difference between *watch* and *follow.* (1 **SD 94a**)
5. *one of them lost his temper* (l. 29). Write sentences using the following: *in a good temper, in a good mood, in a bad temper* and *in the mood.* (1 **SD 206**)

Multiple Choice Questions

a Choose the one answer (A, B, C or D) which you think is correct in the following:
How did one of the workmen get permission to make a telephone call?

A He admitted that he was a student;
B He said he really was a workman;
C He spoke to the police seriously and asked for permission to make a call;
D He said that a policeman could come with him to the call-box.

b Choose the two answers which you think are correct in the following:
Only then . . . that it had been a trick.

A he realized B he understood C did he realize D did he understand E he did realize

Unit 3

INSTRUCTIONS TO THE STUDENT

No language exercises have been included in Unit 3. You should now be able to write continuous English prose entirely on your own.

How to Work
Carry out the detailed instructions given in the Introduction to Unit 2 (p. 56). They are very important. Here is a brief summary:

Comprehension
Write complete answers in your own words as far as possible.

Vocabulary
Explain each word or phrase as it is used in the passage.

Précis
Make out a list of Points, a Rough Draft, and a Fair Copy. Do not exceed the word limit. At the end of your Fair Copy write the number of words you have used.

Composition
Make out a full plan which contains an Introduction, a Development and a Conclusion. Write essays of about 300 words in three or four paragraphs.

Letter-writing
Pay close attention to the Layout of each letter. Answer each question closely. Do not exceed the word limit.

Example
Work carefully through this past Lower Certificate paper. Note how the questions have been answered.

Read carefully the following passage and answer questions *i*, *ii* and *iii*.

As I stepped out of the train I felt unusually solitary, since I was the only passenger to alight. I was accustomed to arriving in the summer, when holiday makers throng coastal resorts, and this was my first visit when the season was over. My destination was a little village eight miles distant by the road, but only four if you took the cliff path over the moor. This I always did, unless it was raining: and I left my luggage at the bus office beside the railway station, to be conveyed for me on the next bus, so that I could enjoy my walk unhampered by a suitcase.

It took me only a few minutes to come to the foot of the cliff path. Half way up I paused to enjoy the sight of the purple hills stretching away to my right and to my left the open sea. When I reached the top I had left all signs of habitation behind me. The moorland turf was springy under my feet, the air was like wine and I felt rejuvenated and intoxicated with it. Glancing seaward a minute or two later, I was surprised to notice that the sky was already aflame with the sunset. The air grew perceptibly cooler and I began to look forward to the delectable hot meal I should have when I reached the inn. It seemed to be getting dark amazingly quickly. I did not think that I had walked unduly slowly and I was at a loss to account for the exceptionally early end of daylight, until I recollected that on previous visits I had walked in high summer and now it was October and the nights were drawing in.

20   All at once it was night. The track was grassy and even in daylight showed up hardly at all against the moor, so it was difficult to keep on it now. If only I had been a smoker with matches always to hand, or if my torch had been in my pocket instead of in the suitcase, I could have walked with more assurance. As it was, I was terrified of hurtling over the edge of the cliff to the rocks below.

25 When I did stray, however, it was towards the hills. I felt my feet squelching and sticking in something soggy. There was no bog to my knowledge near the track, so I must have wandered a long way off my course. I extricated myself with difficulty and very cautiously edged myself towards the sound of the sea. Then I bumped into a little clump of trees that suddenly loomed up in front of

30 me. This was providential rest and shelter until the moon rose. I climbed up the nearest trunk and managed to find a tolerably comfortable fork in which to sit. The waiting seemed interminable and was relieved only by my attempts to identify the little stirrings and noises of animal life that I could hear. I grew colder and colder and managed to sleep only in uneasy, fitful starts, waking

35 when my position got cramped. At last, when the moon came up, I discovered that I was not more than fifty yards from the track and I was soon on my way again.

i Give short answers to each of the following questions, in your own words as far as possible, using only material contained in the passage. Use *one* complete sentence for each answer.

a How was the author's arrival at the station this time different from his arrival on other occasions?

b Why did the author leave his luggage in the bus office?

c Why was the author surprised at the darkness coming so soon?

ii Choose *five* of the following words and phrases and give for each another word or phrase of similar meaning to that in which the word or phrase is used in the passage: coastal resorts (l. 3); all signs of habitation (l. 10); rejuvenated (l. 12); glancing seaward (l. 12); perceptibly (l. 14); unduly (l. 16); account for (l. 17); recollected (l. 17).

iii Give an account *in not more than 80 words* of the author's experiences on the moor after it had become completely dark. Use your own words as far as possible. Do not include anything that is not in the last paragraph.

Possible Answers

i Comprehension

a The author's arrival at the station this time was different from his arrival on other occasions because this was the first time he had ever visited the coastal resort after the holiday season had passed.

b The author left his luggage in the bus office so that he could enjoy his walk without having to carry anything.

c The author was surprised at the darkness coming so soon because at first he failed to realize that the days were now shorter because summer had passed.

ii Vocabulary
coastal resorts: places near the sea-shore where people spend their holidays.
rejuvenated: young again.
perceptibly: noticeably.
unduly: excessively.
recollected: remembered.

iii Précis
Points (The author's experiences)
1. Difficult to keep on track.
2. Strayed—hills.
3. Feet stuck—something soggy.
4. Off course.
5. Extricated himself.
6. Went—sound of sea.
7. Bumped—clump of trees.
8. Climbed nearest trunk.
9. Sat in fork.
10. Waited—long time.
11. Felt cold.
12. Slept—fitful starts.
13. Moon rose—able to see track.
14. Continued his way.

Rough Draft (Joining the Points)
In the darkness, the author could not follow the track and wandered towards the hills. When he got stuck in soggy soil, he knew he had lost his way. After extricating himself, he walked towards the sound of the sea. It was then that he bumped into a clump of trees so he climbed up the nearest trunk and sat in a branch. He waited there for a long time, and even though he felt very cold, he slept for short intervals. When the moon rose, he was able to see the track a short way off and he continued his way.
(102 words)

Fair Copy (Corrected Draft)
Unable to follow the track in the darkness, the author wandered off his course towards the hills where he got stuck in a bog. After extricating himself, he walked towards the sea. When he bumped into a clump of trees, he climbed up the nearest trunk, sat on a branch and waited there a long time. Though he felt cold, he managed to get a little sleep. Later, when the moon rose, he saw the track and continued his way.   (80 words)

Key Structures and Special Difficulties
In this exercise you will be asked to rewrite a sentence taken from the passage without changing its meaning. This exercise tests your ability to use your English to express yourself in a restricted way.

Multiple Choice Questions
You will again find comprehension questions in which you are asked to choose the correct answer from a number of suggested answers. This exercise tests your ability to understand the meaning of the passage you have read and also to recognize grammatical errors in English.

41 Illusions of Pastoral Peace

The quiet life of the country has never appealed to me. City born and city bred, I have always regarded the country as something you look at through a train
5 window, or something you occasionally visit during the week-end. Most of my friends live in the city, yet they always go into raptures at the mere mention of the country. Though they extol the virtues of
10 the peaceful life, only one of them has ever gone to live in the country and he was back in town within six months. Even he still lives under the illusion that country life is somehow superior to town
15 life. He is forever talking about the friendly people, the clean atmosphere,

the gentle pace of living

the closeness to nature and the gentle pace of living. Nothing can be compared, he maintains, with the first cock crow, the twittering of birds at dawn, the sight of the rising sun glinting on the trees and pastures. This idyllic pastoral scene is
20 only part of the picture. My friend fails to mention the long and friendless winter evenings which are interrupted only by an occasional visit to the local cinema—virtually the only form of entertainment. He says nothing about the poor selection of goods in the shops, or about those unfortunate people who have to travel from the country to the city every day to get to work. Why people are
25 prepared to tolerate a four hour journey each day for the dubious privilege of living in the country is beyond my ken. They could be saved so much misery and expense if they chose to live in the city where they rightly belong.

If you can do without the few pastoral pleasures of the country, you will find the city can provide you with the best that life can offer. You never have to
30 travel miles to see your friends. They invariably live nearby and are always available for an informal chat or an evening's entertainment. Some of my acquaintances in the country come up to town once or twice a year to visit the theatre as a special treat. For them this is a major operation which involves considerable planning. As the play draws to its close, they wonder whether they
35 will ever catch that last train home. The city dweller never experiences anxieties of this sort. The latest exhibitions, films, or plays are only a short bus ride away. Shopping, too, is always a pleasure. There is so much variety that you never have to make do with second best. Country people run wild when they go shopping in the city and stagger home loaded with as many of the necessities of life as
40 they can carry. Nor is the city without its moments of beauty. There is something comforting about the warm glow shed by advertisements on cold wet winter nights. Few things could be more impressive than the peace that descends on deserted city streets at week-ends when the thousands that travel to work every day are tucked away in their homes in the country. It has always been a mystery
45 to me why city dwellers, who appreciate all these things, obstinately pretend that they would prefer to live in the country.

Comprehension

Give short answers to these questions in your own words as far as possible. Use one complete sentence for each answer.
a How long did one of the author's city friends live in the country?
b Why does the author find fault with his friend's description of the country?
c Why does the author consider people who have to travel from the country to the city every day unfortunate?

Vocabulary

Explain the meanings of the following words and phrases as they are used in the passage: extol the virtues (l. 9); illusion (l. 13); superior to (l. 14); maintains (l. 18); glinting (l. 19); tolerate (l. 25); beyond my ken (l. 26).

Précis

In not more than 80 words give an account of the advantages which the author attributes to living in the city. Use your own words as far as possible. Do not include anything that is not in the last paragraph.

Composition

Write a composition in about 300 words on one of the following:
a Write an answer to the above passage pointing out the advantages of living in the country and the disadvantages of living in the city.
b Which part of your country would you prefer to live in?

Letter-writing

A friend of yours who lives in the country intends to come to town for a few days and has written to you asking if you could put him up. Write him a letter of about 100 words offering him the use of your guest room.

Key Structures and Special Difficulties

Rewrite the following sentence without changing the meaning. Then refer to ll. 24–26.
I can't understand why people are prepared to tolerate a four hour journey each day for the dubious privilege of living in the country.
Why people . . .

Multiple Choice Questions

a Choose the answer (A, B, C or D) which you think is correct in the following:
When a city dweller goes shopping he is lucky because:
A the city shops are very big;
B shopping is a pleasure;
C there is a lot of variety so you can choose exactly what you want;
D there is a poor selection of goods in the shops.

b Choose the two answers which you think are correct in each of the following:
1. *For country people, a visit to the theatre is a special . . .*
A event B situation C condition D occasion E action
2. *They could be saved . . . misery and expense if they chose to live in the city.*
A so B such C such a D a such E so much

42 Modern Cavemen

Cave exploration, or potholing, as it has
come to be known, is a relatively new
sport. Perhaps it is the desire for solitude
or the chance of making an unexpected
5 discovery that lures men down to the
depths of the earth. It is impossible to
give a satisfactory explanation for a potholer's motives. For him, caves have the
same peculiar fascination which high
10 mountains have for the climber. They
arouse instincts which can only be dimly
understood.

... *can only be dimly understood*

Exploring really deep caves is not a
task for the Sunday afternoon rambler.
15 Such undertakings require the precise
planning and foresight of military opera-
tions. It can take as long as eight days to rig up rope ladders and to establish
supply bases before a descent can be made into a very deep cave. Precautions of
this sort are necessary, for it is impossible to foretell the exact nature of the
20 difficulties which will confront the potholer. The deepest known cave in the
world is the Gouffre Berger near Grenoble. It extends to a depth of 3723 feet.
This immense chasm has been formed by an underground stream which has
tunnelled a course through a flaw in the rocks. The entrance to the cave is on a
plateau in the Dauphiné Alps. As it is only six feet across, it is barely noticeable.
25 The cave might never have been discovered had not the entrance been spotted
by the distinguished French potholer, Berger. Since its discovery, it has become
a sort of potholers' Everest. Though a number of descents have been made,
much of it still remains to be explored.

A team of potholers recently went down the Gouffre Berger. After entering
30 the narrow gap on the plateau, they climbed down the steep sides of the cave
until they came to a narrow corridor. They had to edge their way along this,
sometimes wading across shallow streams, or swimming across deep pools.
Suddenly they came to a waterfall which dropped into an underground lake at
the bottom of the cave They plunged into the lake, and after loading their gear
35 on an inflatable rubber dinghy, let the current carry them to the other side. To
protect themselves from the icy water, they had to wear special rubber suits.
At the far end of the lake, they came to huge piles of rubble which had been
washed up by the water. In this part of the cave, they could hear an insistent
booming sound which they found was caused by a small water-spout shooting
40 down into a pool from the roof of the cave. Squeezing through a cleft in the
rocks, the potholers arrived at an enormous cavern, the size of a huge concert
hall. After switching on powerful arc lights, they saw great stalagmites—some
of them over forty feet high—rising up like tree-trunks to meet the stalactites
suspended from the roof. Round about, piles of lime-stone glistened in all the
45 colours of the rainbow. In the eerie silence of the cavern, the only sound that
could be heard was made by water which dripped continuously from the high
dome above them.

Comprehension

Give short answers to these questions in your own words as far as possible. Use one complete sentence for each answer.
a Why does the exploration of a deep cave require careful planning?
b How has the Gouffre Berger been formed?
c Why might the entrance to the Gouffre Berger never have been discovered?

Vocabulary

Explain the meanings of the following words and phrases as they are used in the passage: relatively (l. 2); desire for solitude (l. 3); lures (l. 5); arouse (l. 11); precise (l. 15); confront (l. 20); is barely noticeable (l. 24).

Précis

Give an account *in not more than 80 words* of the potholers' experiences after they entered the Gouffre Berger. Use your own words as far as possible. Do not include anything that is not in the last paragraph.

Composition

Write a composition in about 300 words on one of the following:
a Describe a man's efforts to escape from a cave by the sea-shore in order to avoid the incoming tide.
b The most popular sport in your country.

Letter-writing

You had a party at your home recently but unintentionally neglected to invite a close friend of yours. Write him a letter of about 100 words apologizing for this and explaining how the mistake came about.

Key Structures and Special Difficulties

Rewrite the following sentence without changing the meaning. Then refer to ll. 38–40.
   The insistent booming sound they could hear was found to be caused by a small water-spout shooting down into a pool from the roof of the cave.
   They could hear . . . which they . . .

Multiple Choice Questions

a Choose the one answer (A, B, C or D) which you think is correct in the following:
   How did the potholers get across the lake inside the Gouffre Berger?
   A   By swimming;
   B   By rowing across in a rubber dinghy;
   C   By letting the current carry them to the other side;
   D   By wading.

b Choose the two answers which you think are correct in each of the following:

   1. *After . . . the narrow gap, they climbed down the steep sides of the cave.*
   A they were entering   B they had entered   C entering   D entered   E they will enter

   2. *They could hear the water booming . . . in this part of the cave.*
   A continually   B now and again   C frequently   D continuously   E all the time

43 Fully Insured

Insurance companies are normally willing to insure anything. Insuring public or private property is a standard practice in most countries in the world. If, however,
5 you were holding an open air garden party or a fête it would be equally possible to insure yourself in the event of bad weather. Needless to say, the bigger the risk an insurance company takes, the
10 higher the premium you will have to pay. It is not uncommon to hear that a shipping company has made a claim for the cost of salvaging a sunken ship. But the claim made by a local authority to recover
15 the cost of salvaging a sunken pie dish must surely be unique.

it was an unusual pie dish

  Admittedly it was an unusual pie dish, for it was eighteen feet long and six feet wide. It had been purchased by a local authority so that an enormous pie could be baked for an annual fair. The pie committee decided that the best way
20 to transport the dish would be by canal, so they insured it for the trip. Shortly after it was launched, the pie committee went to a local inn to celebrate. At the same time, a number of teenagers climbed on to the dish and held a little party of their own. Modern dances proved to be more than the dish could bear, for during the party it capsized and sank in seven feet of water.
25   The pie committee telephoned a local garage owner who arrived in a recovery truck to salvage the pie dish. Shivering in their wet clothes, the teenagers looked on while three men dived repeatedly into the water to locate the dish. They had little difficulty in finding it, but hauling it out of the water proved to be a serious problem. The sides of the dish were so smooth that it was almost
30 impossible to attach hawsers and chains to the rim without damaging it. Eventually chains were fixed to one end of the dish and a powerful winch was put into operation. The dish rose to the surface and was gently drawn towards the canal bank. For one agonizing moment, the dish was perched precariously on the bank of the canal, but it suddenly overbalanced and slid back into the water.
35 The men were now obliged to try once more. This time they fixed heavy metal clamps to both sides of the dish so that they could fasten the chains. The dish now had to be lifted vertically because one edge was resting against the side of the canal. The winch was again put into operation and one of the men started up the truck. Several minutes later, the dish was successfully hauled above the
40 surface of the water. Water streamed in torrents over its sides with such force that it set up a huge wave in the canal. There was danger that the wave would rebound off the other side of the bank and send the dish plunging into the water again. By working at tremendous speed, the men managed to get the dish on to dry land before the wave returned.

Comprehension

Give short answers to these questions in your own words as far as possible. Use one complete sentence for each answer.
a How is a policy-holder affected when an insurance company takes a big risk?
b Why had the local authorities bought such a big pie dish?
c Why did the pie dish capsize?

Vocabulary

Explain the meanings of the following words and phrases as they are used in the passage: a standard practice (l. 3); in the event of (l. 7); premium (l. 10); salvaging (l. 15); annual (l. 19); launched (l. 21); capsized (l. 24).

Précis

Describe *in not more than 80 words* how the pie dish was recovered after it had been located in the water. Use your own words as far as possible. Do not include anything that is not in the last paragraph.

Composition

Write a composition in about 300 words on one of the following:
a Write an imaginary account of how the pie dish capsized during the party held by the teenagers.
b Describe a day spent by the river or by the sea.

Letter-writing

You have just heard that a friend of yours was recently involved in a car accident but was not hurt. Write a letter of about 100 words telling him how you came to hear of the accident and expressing the hope that he has recovered from his unpleasant experience.

Key Structures and Special Difficulties

Rewrite the following sentence without changing the meaning. Then refer to ll. 35–36.
   This time heavy metal clamps were fixed to both sides of the dish so that the chains could be fastened.
   This time they . . .

Multiple Choice Questions

a Choose the one answer (A, B, C or D) which you think is correct in the following:
   The huge wave in the canal was caused by:
A the sinking of the pie dish;
B the dish sliding back into the water;
C the great quantity of water which poured off the dish when they were getting it out;
D the party of teenagers.

b Choose the two answers which you think are correct in each of the following:
   1. *The cold water made the teenagers . . .*
   A tremble B to tremble C shake D shiver E to shiver
   2. *It was . . . for the three men to find the pie dish.*
   A easy B difficult C ease D difficulty E simple

44 Speed and Comfort

People travelling long distances frequently have to decide whether they
would prefer to go by land, sea, or air.
Hardly anyone can positively enjoy sitting
5 in a train for more than a few hours.
Train compartments soon get cramped
and stuffy. It is almost impossible to take
your mind off the journey. Reading is
only a partial solution, for the monotonous
10 rhythm of the wheels clicking on the
rails soon lulls you to sleep. During the
day, sleep comes in snatches. At night,
when you really wish to go to sleep, you
rarely manage to do so. If you are lucky
15 enough to get a couchette, you spend half
the night staring at the small blue light

. . . meet interesting people

in the ceiling, or fumbling to find your passport when you cross a frontier.
Inevitably you arrive at your destination almost exhausted. Long car journeys
are even less pleasant, for it is quite impossible even to read. On motor-ways you
20 can, at least, travel fairly safely at high speeds, but more often than not, the
greater part of the journey is spent on narrow, bumpy roads which are crowded
with traffic. By comparison, trips by sea offer a great variety of civilized com-
forts. You can stretch your legs on the spacious decks, play games, swim, meet
interesting people and enjoy good food—always assuming, of course, that the
25 sea is calm. If it is not, and you are likely to get sea-sick, no form of transport
could be worse. Even if you travel in ideal weather, sea journeys take a long
time. Relatively few people are prepared to sacrifice up to a third of their holidays
for the pleasure of travelling on a ship.
Aeroplanes have the reputation of being dangerous and even hardened travel-
30 lers are intimidated by them. They also have the grave disadvantage of being
the most expensive form of transport. But nothing can match them for speed
and comfort. Travelling at a height of 30,000 feet, far above the clouds, and at
over 500 miles an hour is an exhilarating experience. You do not have to devise
ways of taking your mind off the journey, for an aeroplane gets you to your
35 destination rapidly. For a few hours, you settle back in a deep armchair to enjoy
the flight. The real escapist can watch a free film show and sip champagne on
some services. But even when such refinements are not available, there is plenty
to keep you occupied. An aeroplane offers you an unusual and breathtaking
view of the world. You soar effortlessly over high mountains and deep valleys.
40 You really see the shape of the land. If the landscape is hidden from view, you
can enjoy the extraordinary sight of unbroken cloud plains that stretch out for
miles before you, while the sun shines brilliantly in a clear sky. The journey is
so smooth that there is nothing to prevent you from reading or sleeping. However you decide to spend your time, one thing is certain: you will arrive at your
45 destination fresh and uncrumpled. You will not have to spend the next few days
recovering from a long and arduous journey.

Comprehension

Give short answers to these questions in your own words as far as possible. Use one complete sentence for each answer.

a Why is it difficult to read on a train?
b What makes long car journeys unpleasant?
c What are the two disadvantages of travelling by sea?

Vocabulary

Explain the meanings of the following words and phrases as they are used in the passage: cramped and stuffy (ll. 6–7); monotonous (l. 9); lulls (l. 11); in snatches (l. 12); destination (l. 18); stretch your legs (l. 23); sacrifice (l. 27).

Précis

In not more than 80 words give an account of the advantages of travelling by air. Use your own words as far as possible. Do not include anything that is not in the last paragraph.

Composition

Write a composition in about 300 words on one of the following:

a Which form of transport do you prefer for long distance journeys: train, car, or ship?
b The disadvantages of travelling by air.

Letter-writing

You had bought a ticket to the theatre but now find that you will be unable to go. Write a letter of about 100 words to a friend enclosing the ticket and explaining why you are sending it to him.

Key Structures and Special Difficulties

Rewrite the following sentence without changing the meaning. Then refer to ll. 42–43.

You travel so smoothly that there is nothing to prevent you from reading or sleeping.
The journey . . .

Multiple Choice Questions

a Choose the one answer (A, B, C or D) which you think is correct in the following:
Some people object to air travel because they claim:

A   you can't see anything while travelling;
B   you get airsick;
C   you take too great a risk;
D   aeroplanes fly too quickly and this is dangerous.

b Choose the two answers which you think are correct in each of the following:

1. *. . . you decide to spend your time, one thing is certain: you will arrive at your destination fresh and uncrumpled.*

A Whenever   B Wherever   C No matter how   D Whoever   E In whatever way

2. *Nothing can . . . aeroplanes for speed and comfort.*

A match with   B compare with   C equal   D equal with   E equal to

45 The Power of the Press

In democratic countries any efforts to restrict the freedom of the Press are rightly condemned. However, this freedom can easily be abused. Stories about
5 people often attract far more public attention than political events. Though we may enjoy reading about the lives of others, it is extremely doubtful whether we would equally enjoy reading about
10 ourselves. Acting on the contention that facts are sacred, reporters can cause untold suffering to individuals by publishing details about their private lives. Newspapers exert such tremendous in-
15 fluence that they can not only bring about major changes to the lives of ordinary people but can even overthrow a government.

The rise to fame was swift

The story of a poor family that acquired fame and fortune overnight, dramatically illustrates the power of the press. The family lived in Aberdeen, a small
20 town of 23,000 inhabitants in South Dakota. As the parents had five children, life was a perpetual struggle against poverty. They were expecting their sixth child and were faced with even more pressing economic problems. If they had only had one more child, the fact would have passed unnoticed. They would have continued to struggle against economic odds and would have lived in
25 obscurity. But they suddenly became the parents of quintuplets, four girls and a boy, an event which radically changed their lives. The day after the birth of the five children, an aeroplane arrived in Aberdeen bringing sixty reporters and photographers. The news was of national importance, for the poor couple had become the parents of the only quintuplets in America.
30 The rise to fame was swift. Television cameras and newspapers carried the news to everyone in the country. Newspapers and magazines offered the family huge sums for the exclusive rights to publish stories and photographs. Gifts poured in not only from unknown people, but from baby food and soap manufacturers who wished to advertise their products. The old farmhouse the family
35 lived in was to be replaced by a new $100,000 home. Reporters kept pressing for interviews so lawyers had to be employed to act as spokesmen for the family at press conferences. The event brought serious changes to the town itself. Plans were announced to build a huge new highway, as Aberdeen was now likely to attract thousands of tourists. Signposts erected on the outskirts of the town
40 directed tourists not to Aberdeen, but to 'Quint-City U.S.A.' The local authorities discussed the possibility of erecting a 'quint museum' to satisfy the curiosity of the public and to protect the family from inquisitive tourists. While the five babies were still quietly sleeping in oxygen tents in a hospital nursery, their parents were paying the price for fame. It would never again be possible
45 for them to lead normal lives. They had become the victims of commercialization, for their names had acquired a market value. The town itself received so

much attention that almost every one of the inhabitants was affected to a greater or less degree.

Comprehension

Give short answers to these questions in your own words as far as possible. Use one complete sentence for each answer.
a How can newspapermen cause untold suffering to ordinary people?
b What event made the poor family in South Dakota famous?
c What happened the day after the birth of the children?

Vocabulary

Explain the meanings of the following words and phrases as they are used in the passage: restrict (l. 2); equally (l. 9); contention (l. 10); untold (l. 12); acquired (l. 18); perpetual struggle (l. 21); in obscurity (ll. 24–25).

Précis

Describe *in not more than 80 words* how the birth of the five children affected the family and the town. Use your own words as far as possible. Do not include anything that is not in the last paragraph.

Composition

Write a composition in about 300 words on one of the following:
a Write a 'human interest' story about a person who suddenly acquired fame because he won a lot of money from football pools.
b Describe the newspaper you most enjoy reading.

Letter-writing

Write a letter of about 100 words to the Editor of a newspaper complaining about an article that was published recently. Begin 'Dear Sir' and end 'Yours faithfully'.

Key Structures and Special Difficulties

Rewrite the following sentence without changing the meaning. Then refer to ll. 31–32.
The family were offered huge sums by newspapers and magazines.
Newspapers and magazines . . .

Multiple Choice Questions

a Choose the one answer (A, B, C or D) which you think is correct in the following:
Tourists were sure to come to Aberdeen.

A   That was why the local authorities planned to build a new road;
B   That was why the five babies were kept in oxygen tents;
C   That was why the family were going to move to a new $100,000 home;
D   That was why lawyers had to be employed to protect the family.

b Choose the two answers which you think are correct in the following:
Reporters . . . pressing for interviews so lawyers had to be employed.

A wanted   B went on   C kept in   D continued   E insisted

46 Do It Yourself

So great is our passion for doing things for ourselves, that we are becoming increasingly less dependent on specialized labour. No one can plead ignorance of a
5 subject any longer, for there are countless do-it-yourself publications. Armed with the right tools and materials, newly-weds gaily embark on the task of decorating their own homes. Men of all ages spend
10 hours of their leisure time installing their own fireplaces, laying-out their own gardens; building garages and making furniture. Some really keen enthusiasts go so far as to build their own record
15 players and radio transmitters. Shops cater for the do-it-yourself craze not only

wives assume their husbands will put things right

by running special advisory services for novices, but by offering consumers bits and pieces which they can assemble at home. Such things provide an excellent outlet for pent-up creative energy, but unfortunately not all of us are born
20 handymen.

Wives tend to believe that their husbands are infinitely resourceful and versatile. Even husbands who can hardly drive a nail in straight are supposed to be born electricians, carpenters, plumbers and mechanics. When lights fuse, furniture gets rickety, pipes get clogged, or vacuum cleaners fail to operate,
25 wives automatically assume that their husbands will somehow put things right. The worst thing about the do-it-yourself game is that sometimes husbands live under the delusion that they can do anything even when they have been repeatedly proved wrong. It is a question of pride as much as anything else.

Last spring my wife suggested that I call in a man to look at our lawn-mower.
30 It had broken down the previous summer, and though I promised to repair it, I had never got round to it. I would not hear of the suggestion and said that I would fix it myself. One Saturday afternoon, I hauled the machine into the garden and had a close look at it. As far as I could see, it only needed a minor adjustment: a turn of a screw here, a little tightening up there, a drop of oil
35 and it would be as good as new. Inevitably the repair job was not quite so simple. The mower firmly refused to mow, so I decided to dismantle it. The garden was soon littered with chunks of metal which had once made up a lawn-mower. But I was extremely pleased with myself. I had traced the cause of the trouble. One of the links in the chain that drives the wheels had snapped. After buying a new
40 chain I was faced with the insurmountable task of putting the confusing jigsaw puzzle together again. I was not surprised to find that the machine still refused to work after I had reassembled it, for the simple reason that I was left with several curiously shaped bits of metal which did not seem to fit anywhere. I gave up in despair. The weeks passed and the grass grew. When my wife nagged
45 me to do something about it, I told her that either I would have to buy a new mower or let the grass grow. Needless to say our house is now surrounded by a

jungle. Buried somewhere in deep grass there is a rusting lawn-mower which I have promised to repair one day.

Comprehension

Give short answers to these questions in your own words as far as possible. Use one complete sentence for each answer.
a Why do we not rely on specialized labour so much nowadays?
b How do shops encourage people to do things for themselves?
c What do wives tend to believe about their husbands?

Vocabulary

Explain the meanings of the following words and phrases as they are used in the passage: increasingly (ll. 2–3); plead ignorance (l. 4); gaily embark on the task (l. 8); installing (l. 10); novices (l. 17); versatile (l. 22); repeatedly (ll. 27–28).

Précis

Describe *in not more than 80 words* the author's efforts to repair his lawn-mower. Use your own words as far as possible. Do not include anything that is not in the last paragraph.

Composition

Write a composition in about 300 words on one of the following:
a Describe a similar 'do-it-yourself' experience of your own.
b Your favourite hobby.

Letter-writing

Write a letter of about 100 words to an uncle who gave you some good advice two years ago which you acted on. This enabled you to do very well in your work. Thank him and give news of yourself.

Key Structures and Special Difficulties

Rewrite the following sentence without changing the meaning. Then refer to ll. 31–32.
'*I shall fix it myself,*' I said.
I said that . . .

Multiple Choice Questions

a Choose the one answer (A, B, C or D) which you think is correct in the following:
The writer made a few minor adjustments first. What effect did this have?
A The mower got worse;
B No effect at all;
C The mower firmly refused to mow;
D The mower was as good as new.

b Choose the two answers which you think are correct in the following:
. . . what I did, our house is now surrounded by a jungle.
A in addition to   B However,   C As a result of   D The effect of   E Because of

47 Through the Earth's Crust

Satellites orbiting round the earth have provided scientists with a vast amount of information about conditions in outer space. By comparison, relatively little is
5 known about the internal structure of the earth. It has proved easier to go up than to go down. The deepest hole ever to be bored on land went down 25,340 feet—considerably less than the height of
10 Mount Everest. Drilling a hole under the sea has proved to be even more difficult. The deepest hole bored under sea has been about 20,000 feet. Until recently, scientists have been unable to devise a
15 drill which would be capable of cutting through hard rock at great depths.

This problem has now been solved . . .

This problem has now been solved. Scientists have developed a method which sounds surprisingly simple. A new drill which is being tested at Leona Valley Ranch in Texas is driven by a turbine engine which is propelled by liquid mud
20 pumped into it from the surface. As the diamond tip of the drill revolves, it is lubricated by mud. Scientists have been amazed to find that it can cut through the hardest rock with great ease. The drill has been designed to bore through the earth to a depth of 35,000 feet. It will enable scientists to obtain samples of the mysterious layer which lies immediately below the earth's crust. This layer
25 is known as the Mohorovicic Discontinuity, but is commonly referred to as 'the Moho'.

Before it is possible to drill this deep hole, scientists will have to overcome a number of problems. Geological tests will be carried out to find the point at which the earth's crust is thinnest. The three possible sites which are being
30 considered are all at sea: two in the Atlantic Ocean and one in the Pacific. Once they have determined on a site, they will have to erect a drilling vessel which will not be swept away by ocean currents. The vessel will consist of an immense platform which will rise to 70 feet above the water. It will be supported by six hollow columns which will descend to a depth of 60 feet below the ocean surface
35 where they will be fixed to a huge float. A tall steel tower rising to a height of nearly 200 feet will rest on the platform. The drill will be stored in the tower and will have to be lowered through about 15,000 feet of water before operations can begin. Within the tower, there will be a laboratory, living accommodation and a helicopter landing station. Keeping the platform in position at sea will
40 give rise to further problems. To do this, scientists will have to devise methods using radar and underwater television. If, during the operations the drill has to be withdrawn, it must be possible to re-insert it. Great care will therefore have to be taken to keep the platform steady and make it strong enough to withstand hurricanes. If the project is successful, scientists will not only learn a great deal
45 about the earth, but possibly about the nature of the universe itself.

Comprehension

Give short answers to these questions in your own words as far as possible. Use one complete sentence for each answer.
a Why do scientists know relatively little about the interior of the earth?
b What has prevented them from boring to great depths up to now?
c What has enabled the new drill to cut through the hardest rock?

Vocabulary

Explain the meanings of the following words and phrases as they are used in the passages: orbiting (l. 1); vast (l. 2); internal structure (l. 5); devise (l. 14); propelled (l. 19); revolves (l. 20); obtain samples (l. 23).

Précis

In not more than 80 words describe what scientists will have to do to drill a hole through the earth's crust. Use your own words as far as possible. Do not include anything that is not in the last paragraph.

Composition

Write a composition in about 300 words on one of the following:
a Describe an imaginary journey by submarine.
b Recent advances in undersea exploration.

Letter-writing

In not more than 100 words write a letter which you would very much like to receive.

Key Structures and Special Difficulties

Rewrite the following sentence without changing the meaning. Then refer to ll. 29–30.
They are considering three possible sites which are all at sea.
The three . . . which are . . .

Multiple Choice Questions

a Choose the one answer (A, B, C or D) which you think is correct in the following:
It won't be possible to make preparations for drilling the hole until:

A   an immense platform is erected;
B   a tall tower rising to 200 feet is built;
C   a helicopter landing station is built;
D   scientists decide on the best site.

b Choose the two answers which you think are correct in the following:

1. *During operations the drill might have to be withdrawn . . . it must be possible to re-insert it.*

A if   B unless   C so   D therefore   E after

2. *Keeping the platform in position at sea . . . further problems.*

A caused   B will cause   C will create   D had created   E created

48   The Silent Village

In this much-travelled world, there are still thousands of places which are inaccessible to tourists. We always assume that villagers in remote places are friendly
5 and hospitable. But people who are cut off not only from foreign tourists, but even from their own countrymen can be hostile to travellers. Visits to really remote villages are seldom enjoyable—as my
10 wife and I discovered during a tour through the Balkans.

hostile to travellers

We had spent several days in a small town and visited a number of old churches in the vicinity. These attracted many
15 visitors for they were not only of great architectural interest, but contained a large number of beautifully preserved frescoes as well. On the day before our departure, several bus loads of tourists descended on the town. This was more than we could bear, so we decided to spend our last day exploring the country-
20 side. Taking a path which led out of the town, we crossed a few fields until we came to a dense wood. We expected the path to end abruptly, but we found that it traced its way through the trees. We tramped through the wood for over two hours until we arrived at a deep stream. We could see that the path continued on the other side, but we had no idea how we could get across the stream. Suddenly
25 my wife spotted a boat moored to the bank. In it there was a boatman fast asleep. We gently woke him up and asked him to ferry us to the other side. Though he was reluctant to do so at first, we eventually persuaded him to take us.

The path led to a tiny village perched on the steep sides of a mountain. The place consisted of a straggling unmade road which was lined on either side by
30 small houses. Even under a clear blue sky, the village looked forbidding, as all the houses were built of grey mud bricks. The village seemed deserted, the only sign of life being an ugly-looking black goat tied to a tree on a short length of rope in a field nearby. Sitting down on a dilapidated wooden fence near the field, we opened a couple of tins of sardines and had a picnic lunch. All at once,
35 I noticed that my wife seemed to be filled with alarm. Looking up I saw that we were surrounded by children in rags who were looking at us silently as we ate. We offered them food and spoke to them kindly, but they remained motionless. I concluded that they were simply shy of strangers. When we later walked down the main street of the village, we were followed by a silent procession of children.
40 The village which had seemed deserted, immediately came to life. Faces appeared at windows. Men in shirt sleeves stood outside their houses and glared at us. Old women in black shawls peered at us from door-ways. The most frightening thing of all was that not a sound could be heard. There was no doubt that we were unwelcome visitors. We needed no further warning. Turning back
45 down the main street, we quickened our pace and made our way rapidly towards the stream where we hoped the boatman was waiting.

Comprehension

Give short answers to these questions in your own words as far as possible. Use one complete sentence for each answer.
a Why are visits to really remote villages seldom enjoyable?
b Why did the author and his wife decide to spend their last day exploring the countryside?
c How did the author and his wife get across the stream?

Vocabulary

Explain the meanings of the following words and phrases as they are used in the passage: inaccessible (ll. 2–3); hospitable (l. 5); hostile (l. 7); vicinity (l. 14); end abruptly (l. 21); traced (l. 22); eventually (l. 27).

Précis

Describe *in not more than 80 words* the experiences of the author and his wife when they visited a remote village in the Balkans. Use your own words as far as possible. Do not include anything that is not in the last paragraph.

Composition

Write a composition in about 300 words on one of the following:
a Describe any village you know well.
b Continue the above passage. Imagine the boatman was not waiting for the author and his wife. Describe what happened.

Letter-writing

Write a letter in not more than 100 words to a very old man congratulating him on the occasion of his eighty-fifth birthday.

Key Structures and Special Difficulties

Rewrite the following sentence without changing the meaning. Then refer to l. 40.
Though the village had seemed deserted, it immediately came to life.
The village w . . .

Multiple Choice Questions

a Choose the one answer (A, B, C or D) which you think is correct in the following:
The writer's wife got frightened when

A she noticed she and her husband had been surrounded by silent children;
B she noticed that the village looked forbidding and deserted;
C she noticed that she and her husband were being followed by the children;
D she noticed that she and her husband were not welcome.

b Choose the two answers which you think are correct in each of the following:
1. *The village seemed deserted, the only sign of life . . . an ugly-looking black goat tied to a tree.*

A been B being C was D has been E will be
2. *When the children were offered food they . . .*

A didn't move B accepted it C refused it D ran away E stood quite still

49 The Ideal Servant

*this occasioned great mirth
among the guests*

It is a good thing my aunt Harriet died years ago. If she were alive today she would not be able to air her views on her favourite topic of conversation: domestic
5 servants. Aunt Harriet lived in that leisurely age when servants were employed to do housework. She had a huge, rambling country house called 'The Gables'. She was sentimentally attached
10 to this house, for even though it was far too big for her needs, she persisted in living there long after her husband's death. Before she grew old, aunt Harriet used to entertain lavishly. I often visited
15 The Gables when I was a boy. No matter how many guests were present, the great house was always immaculate. The parquet floors shone like mirrors; highly polished silver was displayed in gleaming glass cabinets; even my uncle's huge collection of books was kept miraculously free from dust. Aunt Harriet presided
20 over an invisible army of servants that continuously scrubbed, cleaned, and polished. She always referred to them as 'the shifting population', for they came and went with such frequency that I never even got a chance to learn their names. Though my aunt pursued what was, in those days, an enlightened policy in that she never allowed her domestic staff to work more than eight hours a day, she
25 was extremely difficult to please. While she always decried the fickleness of human nature, she carried on an unrelenting search for the ideal servant to the end of her days, even after she had been sadly disillusioned by Bessie.

Bessie worked for aunt Harriet for three years. During that time she so gained my aunt's confidence, that she was put in charge of the domestic staff.
30 Aunt Harriet could not find words to praise Bessie's industry and efficiency. In addition to all her other qualifications, Bessie was an expert cook. She acted the role of the perfect servant for three years before aunt Harriet discovered her 'little weakness'. After being absent from The Gables for a week, my aunt unexpectedly returned one afternoon with a party of guests and instructed
35 Bessie to prepare dinner. Not only was the meal well below the usual standard, but Bessie seemed unable to walk steadily. She bumped into the furniture and kept mumbling about the guests. When she came in with the last course—a huge pudding—she tripped on the carpet and the pudding went flying through the air, narrowly missed my aunt, and crashed on the dining table with con-
40 siderable force. Though this occasioned great mirth among the guests, aunt Harriet was horrified. She reluctantly came to the conclusion that Bessie was drunk. The guests had, of course, realized this from the moment Bessie opened the door for them and, long before the final catastrophe, had had a difficult time trying to conceal their amusement. The poor girl was dismissed instantly.
45 After her departure, aunt Harriet discovered that there were piles of empty wine bottles of all shapes and sizes neatly stacked in what had once been Bessie's wardrobe. They had mysteriously found their way there from the wine-cellar!

Comprehension

Give short answers to these questions in your own words as far as possible. Use one complete sentence for each answer.
a What did aunt Harriet most like to talk about?
b Why did aunt Harriet continue to live in The Gables after her husband's death?
c Why did aunt Harriet always refer to her servants as 'the shifting population'?

Vocabulary

Explain the meanings of the following words and phrases as they are used in the passage: air her views (l. 3); favourite (l. 4); persisted in (l. 11); immaculate (l. 17); invisible (l. 20); enlightened (l. 23); domestic staff (l. 24).

Précis

In not more than 80 words describe what happened after aunt Harriet unexpectedly returned to The Gables with a party of guests. Use your own words as far as possible. Do not include anything that is not in the last paragraph.

Composition

Write a composition in about 300 words on one of the following:
a Write an imaginary account of how Bessie's 'little weakness' went undetected for three years.
b 'It is a good thing that domestic servants have become a great rarity.' What is your opinion?

Letter-writing

Write a letter of thanks to an aunt who has sent you a cheque for £20 for your twenty-first birthday. Say what you intend to do with the money. Do not write more than 100 words.

Key Structures and Special Difficulties

Rewrite the following sentence without changing the meaning. Then refer to ll. 33–34.
My aunt had been absent from The Gables for a week when she unexpectedly returned one afternoon with a party of guests.
After . . . my aunt . . .

Multiple Choice Questions

a Choose the one answer (A, B, C or D) which you think is correct in the following:
Bessie was made responsible for the domestic staff:
A   as a result of her hard work;
B   because she was loyal to my aunt;
C   because she had such good qualifications;
D   because my aunt trusted her.

b Choose the two answers which you think are correct in the following:
1. *Bessie seemed . . . steadily.*
A impossible to walk   B incapable to walk   C incapable of walking   D unable to walk   E not possible for walking
2. *Bessie . . . because she had got drunk.*
A had to apologize   B lost her job   C made aunt Harriet laugh   D threw the pudding at aunt Harriet   E had to leave

50 New Year Resolutions

The New Year is a time for resolutions. Mentally, at least, most of us could compile formidable lists of 'do's' and 'don'ts'. The same old favourites recur year in
5 year out with monotonous regularity. We resolve to get up earlier each morning, eat less, find more time to play with the children, do a thousand and one jobs about the house, be nice to people we
10 don't like, drive carefully, and take the dog for a walk every day. Past experience has taught us that certain accomplishments are beyond attainment. If we remain inveterate smokers, it is only
15 because we have so often experienced the frustration that results from failure. Most

my enthusiasm waned

of us fail in our efforts at self-improvement because our schemes are too ambitious and we never have time to carry them out. We also make the fundamental error of announcing our resolutions to everybody so that we look even more
20 foolish when we slip back into our bad old ways. Aware of these pitfalls, this year I attempted to keep my resolutions to myself. I limited myself to two modest ambitions: to do physical exercises every morning and to read more of an evening. An all-night party on New Year's Eve provided me with a good excuse for not carrying out either of these new resolutions on the first day of the year,
25 but on the second, I applied myself assiduously to the task.

The daily exercises lasted only eleven minutes and I proposed to do them early in the morning before anyone had got up. The self-discipline required to drag myself out of bed eleven minutes earlier than usual was considerable. Nevertheless, I managed to creep down into the living-room for two days before
30 anyone found me out. After jumping about on the carpet and twisting the human frame into uncomfortable positions, I sat down at the breakfast table in an exhausted condition. It was this that betrayed me. The next morning the whole family trooped in to watch the performance. That was really unsettling but I fended off the taunts and jibes of the family good-humouredly and soon
35 everybody got used to the idea. However, my enthusiasm waned. The time I spent at exercises gradually diminished. Little by little the eleven minutes fell to zero. By January 10th, I was back to where I had started from. I argued that if I spent less time exhausting myself at exercises in the morning I would keep my mind fresh for reading when I got home from work. Resisting the hypnotizing
40 effect of television, I sat in my room for a few evenings with my eyes glued to a book. One night, however, feeling cold and lonely, I went downstairs and sat in front of the television pretending to read. That proved to be my undoing, for I soon got back to my old bad habit of dozing off in front of the screen. I still haven't given up my resolution to do more reading. In fact, I have just bought a
45 book entitled 'How to Read a Thousand Words a Minute'. Perhaps it will solve my problem, but I just haven't had time to read it!

Comprehension

Give short answers to these questions in your own words as far as possible. Use one complete sentence for each answer.
a What has past experience of New Year resolutions taught us?
b Why is it a basic mistake to announce our resolutions to everybody?
c Why did the writer not carry out his resolutions on New Year's Day?

Vocabulary

Explain the meanings of the following words and phrases as they are used in the passage: mentally (l. 2); formidable (l. 3); recur year in year out (ll. 4–5); beyond attainment (l. 13); inveterate (l. 14); frustration (l. 16); carrying out (l. 24).

Précis

In not more than 80 words describe the efforts the writer made to carry out his resolutions after New Year's Day. Use your own words as far as possible. Do not include anything that is not in the last paragraph.

Composition

Write a composition in about 300 words on one of the following:
a Write an account of resolutions you have made in the past and failed to keep.
b Describe New Year celebrations in your country.

Letter-writing

Before you went abroad, you promised your parents that you would write once a week. Since then, you have failed to keep your promise. Write a letter to them explaining why it has been impossible for you to write more often. Do not write more than 100 words.

Key Structures and Special Difficulties

Rewrite the following sentence without changing the meaning. Then refer to ll. 45–46.
It may solve my problem, but I just haven't had time to read it!
Perhaps . . .

Multiple Choice Questions

a Choose the one answer (A, B, C or D) which you think is correct in the following:
The writer would have continued doing exercises in the morning if:

A the family hadn't laughed at him;
B he hadn't had to get up eleven minutes earlier than usual;
C this hadn't prevented him from eating his breakfast;
D he hadn't felt so tired by the time he sat down to breakfast.

b Choose the two answers which you think are correct in the following:
1. *He . . . down into the living-room for two days before anyone found him out.*

A could creep   B was able to creep   C succeeded in creeping   D succeeded to creep   E could have crept

2. *After doing exercises for several days, the writer grew . . . enthusiastic.*

A un-   B more and more   C less and less   D fewer and fewer   E in-

51 Automation

One of the greatest advances in modern technology has been the invention of computers. They are already widely used in industry and in universities and the
5 time may come when it will be possible for ordinary people to use them as well. Computers are capable of doing extremely complicated work in all branches of learning. They can solve the most com-
10 plex mathematical problems or put thousands of unrelated facts in order. These machines can be put to varied uses. For instance, they can provide information on the best way to prevent traffic
15 accidents, or they can count the number of times the word 'and' has been used in

*informed about
weather conditions*

the Bible. Because they work accurately and at high speeds, they save research workers years of hard work. This whole process by which machines can be used to work for us has been called *automation*. In the future, automation may enable
20 human beings to enjoy far more leisure than they do today. The coming of automation is bound to have important social consequences.

Some time ago an expert on automation, Sir Leon Bagrit, pointed out that it was a mistake to believe that these machines could 'think'. There is no possibility that human beings will be 'controlled by machines'. Though computers
25 are capable of learning from their mistakes and improving on their performance, they need detailed instructions from human beings in order to be able to operate. They can never, as it were, lead independent lives, or 'rule the world' by making decisions of their own.

Sir Leon said that in the future, computers would be developed which would
30 be small enough to carry in the pocket. Ordinary people would then be able to use them to obtain valuable information. Computers could be plugged into a national network and be used like radios. For instance, people going on holiday could be informed about weather conditions; car drivers could be given alternative routes when there are traffic jams. It will also be possible to make tiny
35 translating machines. This will enable people who do not share a common language to talk to each other without any difficulty or to read foreign publications. It is impossible to assess the importance of a machine of this sort, for many international misunderstandings are caused simply through our failure to understand each other. Computers will also be used in hospitals. By providing
40 a machine with a patient's symptoms, a doctor will be able to diagnose the nature of his illness. Similarly, machines could be used to keep a check on a patient's health record and bring it up to date. Doctors will therefore have immediate access to a great many facts which will help them in their work. Book-keepers and accountants, too, could be relieved of dull clerical work, for
45 the tedious task of compiling and checking lists of figures could be done entirely by machines. Computers are the most efficient servants man has ever had and there is no limit to the way they can be used to improve our lives.

Comprehension

Give short answers to these questions in your own words as far as possible. Use one complete sentence for each answer.

a Why do computers save research workers years of hard work?
b What is automation?
c Why is it a mistake to believe that computers can think?

Vocabulary

Explain the meanings of the following words and phrases as they are used in the passage: widely (l. 3); branches of learning (ll. 8–9); varied (l. 12); leisure (l. 20); bound (l. 21); consequences (l. 21); operate (l. 26).

Précis

In not more than 80 words describe how computers may be used in the future. Use your own words as far as possible. Do not include anything that is not in the last paragraph.

Composition

Write a composition in about 300 words on one of the following:

a A visit to a factory.
b Machines that do housework.

Letter-writing

You have arranged to place your house at the disposal of a friend of yours while you are away on holiday. You are now about to leave. Write him a letter in about 100 words telling him what final arrangements you have made.

Key Structures and Special Difficulties

Rewrite the following sentence without changing the meaning. Then refer to l. 46.

Man has never had such efficient servants as computers.
Computers are . . .

Multiple Choice Questions

a Choose the one answer (A, B, C or D) which you think is correct in the following:
Why will computers be useful to doctors?

A Because they will relieve them of dull clerical work;
B Because they will provide them with information which will help them in their work;
C Because much of the tedious work they have to do will be done entirely by machines;
D Because they are up to date.

b Choose the two answers which you think are correct in each of the following:

1. *If computers were small enough it . . . possible to carry them round in your pocket.*

A would be   B might be   C would have been   D might have been   E were

2. *With the help of computers, motorists would be able to avoid . . . by taking a different road.*

A accidents   B very heavy traffic   C misunderstandings   D bad weather conditions   E traffic jams

52 Mud is Mud

My cousin, Harry, keeps a large curiously shaped bottle on permanent display in his study. Despite the fact that the bottle is tinted a delicate shade of green, an
5 observant visitor would soon notice that it is filled with what looks like a thick, greyish substance. If you were to ask Harry what was in the bottle, he would tell you that it contained perfumed mud.
10 If you expressed doubt or surprise, he would immediately invite you to smell it and then to rub some into your skin. This brief experiment would dispel any further doubts you might entertain. The bottle
15 really does contain perfumed mud. How Harry came into the possession of this

all sorts of weird concoctions

outlandish stuff makes an interesting story which he is fond of relating. Furthermore, the acquisition of this bottle cured him of a bad habit he had been developing for years.

20 Harry used to consider it a great joke to go into expensive cosmetic shops and make outrageous requests for goods that do not exist. He would invent fanciful names on the spot. On entering a shop, he would ask for a new perfume called 'Scented Shadow' or for 'insoluble bath cubes'. If a shop girl told him she had not heard of it, he would pretend to be considerably put out. He loved to be told
25 that one of his imaginary products was temporarily out of stock and he would faithfully promise to call again at some future date, but of course he never did. How Harry managed to keep a straight face during these performances is quite beyond me.

Harry does not need to be prompted to explain how he bought his precious
30 bottle of mud. One day, he went to an exclusive shop in London and asked for 'Myrolite'. The shop assistant looked puzzled and Harry repeated the word, slowly stressing each syllable. When the girl shook her head in bewilderment, Harry went on to explain that 'myrolite' was a hard, amber-like substance which could be used to remove freckles. This explanation evidently conveyed
35 something to the girl who searched shelf after shelf. She produced all sorts of weird concoctions, but none of them met with Harry's requirements. When Harry put on his act of being mildly annoyed, the girl promised to order some for him. Intoxicated by his success, Harry then asked for perfumed mud. He expected the girl to look at him in blank astonishment. However, it was his turn
40 to be surprised, for the girl's eyes immediately lit up and she fetched several bottles which she placed on the counter for Harry to inspect. For once, Harry had to admit defeat. He picked up what seemed to be the smallest bottle and discreetly asked the price. He was glad to get away with a mere five guineas and he beat a hasty retreat, clutching the precious bottle under his arm. From then
45 on, Harry decided that this little game he had invented might prove to be expensive. The curious bottle which now adorns the bookcase in his study was his first and last purchase of rare cosmetics.

Comprehension

Give short answers to these questions in your own words as far as possible. Use one complete sentence for each answer.

a What does the curiously shaped bottle which Harry keeps in his study contain?
b Why did Harry often visit cosmetic shops?
c What would he do when he was told that one of his imaginary products was temporarily out of stock?

Vocabulary

Explain the meanings of the following words and phrases as they are used in the passage: delicate (l. 4); observant (l. 5); entertain (l. 14); came into the possession (l. 16); stuff (l. 17); insoluble (l. 23); to keep a straight face (l. 27); is quite beyond me (ll. 27–28).

Précis

In not more than 80 words describe Harry's experiences on the day he bought a bottle of perfumed mud. Use your own words as far as possible. Do not include anything that is not in the last paragraph.

Composition

Write a composition in about 300 words on one of the following:
a A day's shopping.
b The strangest person I have ever met.

Letter-writing

Your house was damaged during a recent thunderstorm. Write a letter of about 100 words to a friend telling him what happened.

Key Structures and Special Difficulties

Rewrite the following sentence without changing the meaning. Then refer to ll. 33–34.
'"*Myrolite*" *is a hard, amber-like substance and you can use it to remove freckles,*' *Harry went on to explain.*
Harry went on to explain that 'myrolite' . . . which . . .

Multiple Choice Questions

a Choose the one answer (A, B, C or D) which you think is correct in the following:
Harry failed to obtain 'Myrolite':

A because it doesn't exist;
B because they didn't have any in the shop;
C because the girl couldn't understand what he wanted;
D because it was a hard, amber-like substance.

b Choose the two answers which you think are correct in each of the following:
1. *None of the concoctions . . . she produced met with Harry's requirements.*

A who B whom C whose D which E that

2. *Harry stopped playing this practical joke because he was afraid it might* . . .

A get him into trouble B cost him a lot of money C cost him five guineas
D oblige him to spend more than he could afford E annoy people

53 In the Public Interest

The Scandinavian countries are much admired all over the world for their enlightened social policies. Sweden has evolved an excellent system for protecting
5 the individual citizen from high-handed or incompetent public officers. The system has worked so well, that it has been adopted in other countries like Denmark, Norway, Finland, and New Zealand.
10 Even countries with large populations like Britain and the United States are seriously considering imitating the Swedes.

refer to him as the 'J. O.'

The Swedes were the first to recognize
15 that public officials like civil servants, police officers, health inspectors or tax-collectors can make mistakes or act over-zealously in the belief that they are serving the public. As long ago as 1809, the Swedish Parliament introduced a scheme to safeguard the interest of the individual. A parliamentary committee
20 representing all political parties appoints a person who is suitably qualified to investigate private grievances against the State. The official title of the person is 'Justiteombudsman', but the Swedes commonly refer to him as the 'J.O.' or 'Ombudsman'. The Ombudsman is not subject to political pressure. He investigates complaints large and small that come to him from all levels of society.
25 As complaints must be made in writing, the Ombudsman receives an average of 1200 letters a year. He has eight lawyer assistants to help him and he examines every single letter in detail. There is nothing secretive about the Ombudsman's work, for his correspondence is open to public inspection. If a citizen's complaint is justified, the Ombudsman will act on his behalf. The action he takes varies
30 according to the nature of the complaint. He may gently reprimand an official or even suggest to parliament that a law be altered. The following case is a typical example of the Ombudsman's work.

A foreigner living in a Swedish village wrote to the Ombudsman complaining that he had been ill-treated by the police, simply because he was a foreigner.
35 The Ombudsman immediately wrote to the Chief of Police in the district asking him to send a record of the case. There was nothing in the record to show that the foreigner's complaint was justified and the Chief of Police stoutly denied the accusation. It was impossible for the Ombudsman to take action, but when he received a similar complaint from another foreigner in the same village, he
40 immediately sent one of his lawyers to investigate the matter. The lawyer ascertained that a policeman had indeed dealt roughly with foreigners on several occasions. The fact that the policeman was prejudiced against foreigners could not be recorded in the official files. It was only possible for the Ombudsman to find this out by sending one of his representatives to check the facts. The
45 policeman in question was severely reprimanded and was informed that if any further complaints were lodged against him, he would be prosecuted. The

Ombudsman's prompt action at once put an end to an unpleasant practice which might have gone unnoticed.

Comprehension

Give short answers to these questions in your own words as far as possible. Use one complete sentence for each answer.

a Why did Sweden introduce the institution of Ombudsman?
b How is an Ombudsman chosen in Sweden?
c How can the public find out about the Ombudsman's work?

Vocabulary

Explain the meanings of the following words and phrases as they are used in the passage: evolved an excellent system (l. 4); imitating (l. 12); safeguard (l. 19); grievances (l. 21); investigates (l. 24); correspondence (l. 28); altered (l. 31).

Précis

In not more than 80 words write an account of the action the Ombudsman took when he received a complaint from a foreigner in a Swedish village. Use your own words as far as possible. Do not include anything that is not in the last paragraph.

Composition

Write a composition in about 300 words on one of the following:
a Explain whether the Ombudsman institution would be useful in your country.
b Describe the work of any one of the following: a policeman, a civil servant, a health officer, a social worker.

Letter-writing

Write an imaginary letter of about 100 words to an Ombudsman complaining about postal services in your district. Begin 'Dear Sir' and end 'Yours faithfully'.

Key Structures and Special Difficulties

Rewrite the following sentence without changing the meaning. Then refer to ll. 42–43.
The policeman's prejudice against foreigners could not be recorded in the official files.
The fact that . . .

Multiple Choice Questions

a Choose the one answer (A, B, C or D) which you think is correct in the following:
How was the policeman who dealt roughly with foreigners punished?

A He was sent to prison;
B He was prosecuted;
C He was scolded by his superiors;
D He was dismissed from the police force.

b Choose the two answers which you think are correct in the following:
If the Ombudsman hadn't acted promptly this unpleasant practice . . .

A might have continued   B might continue   C will continue   D would continue
E could have continued

54 Instinct or Cleverness?

We have been brought up to fear insects. We regard them as unnecessary creatures that do more harm than good. Man continually wages war on them, for they contaminate his food, carry diseases, or devour his crops. They sting or bite without provocation; they fly uninvited into our rooms on summer nights, or beat against our lighted windows. We live in dread not only of unpleasant insects like spiders or wasps, but of quite harmless ones like moths. Reading about them increases our understanding without dispelling our fears. Knowing that the industrious ant lives in a highly organized society does nothing to prevent

We enjoy staring at them

us from being filled with revulsion when we find hordes of them crawling over a carefully prepared picnic lunch. No matter how much we like honey, or how much we have read about the uncanny sense of direction which bees possess, we have a horror of being stung. Most of our fears are unreasonable, but they are impossible to erase. At the same time, however, insects are strangely fascinating. We enjoy reading about them, especially when we find that, like the praying mantis, they lead perfectly horrible lives. We enjoy staring at them, entranced as they go about their business, unaware (we hope) of our presence. Who has not stood in awe at the sight of a spider pouncing on a fly, or a column of ants triumphantly bearing home an enormous dead beetle?

Last summer I spent days in the garden watching thousands of ants crawling up the trunk of my prize peach tree. The tree has grown against a warm wall on a sheltered side of the house. I am especially proud of it, not only because it has survived several severe winters, but because it occasionally produces luscious peaches. During the summer, I noticed that the leaves of the tree were beginning to wither. Clusters of tiny insects called aphides were to be found on the underside of the leaves. They were visited by a large colony of ants which obtained a sort of honey from them. I immediately embarked on an experiment which, even though it failed to get rid of the ants, kept me fascinated for twenty-four hours. I bound the base of the tree with sticky tape, making it impossible for the ants to reach the aphides. The tape was so sticky that they did not dare to cross it. For a long time, I watched them scurrying around the base of the tree in bewilderment. I even went out at midnight with a torch and noted with satisfaction (and surprise) that the ants were still swarming around the sticky tape without being able to do anything about it. I got up early next morning hoping to find that the ants had given up in despair. Instead, I saw that they had discovered a new route. They were climbing up the wall of the house and then on to the leaves of the tree. I realized sadly that I had been completely defeated by their ingenuity. The ants had been quick to find an answer to my thoroughly unscientific methods!

Comprehension

Give short answers to these questions in your own words as far as possible. Use one complete sentence for each answer.
a What is our attitude to insects?
b Why does man try to exterminate insects?
c What do we enjoy most when reading about insects?

Vocabulary

Explain the meanings of the following words as they are used in the passage: contaminate (l. 5); devour (l. 6); provocation (l. 7); dispelling (l. 14); industrious (l. 15); revulsion (l. 17); pouncing (l. 25).

Précis

Describe *in not more than 80 words* what the writer saw and did when he tried to prevent the ants from climbing up his peach tree. Use your own words as far as possible. Do not include anything that is not in the last paragraph.

Composition

Write a composition in about 300 words on one of the following:
a Write an account of any insect you have read about or observed.
b Describe man's efforts to control pests.

Letter-writing

A friend took some amusing photographs of you when you were on holiday together some time ago. Write him a letter of about 100 words asking him what he has been doing since then and requesting that he send you copies of the photographs he took.

Key Structures and Special Difficulties

Rewrite the following sentence without changing the meaning. Then refer to l. 37.
The tape was sticky and they did not dare to cross it.
The tape was so . . .

Multiple Choice Questions

a Choose the one answer (A, B, C or D) which you think is correct in the following:
What did the author hope when he bound the base of the peach tree with sticky tape?

A   That the ants would stop trying to climb the tree;
B   That the ants would die;
C   That the aphides would die;
D   That the ants would stick to the tape.

b Choose the two answers which you think are correct in each of the following:
1. *A lot of insects . . . on the underside of the leaves.*

A could be found   B could found   C could find   D were to be seen   E might find

2. *The author realized that there was something wrong with the tree when he noticed that the leaves had begun to . . .*

A fall   B turn green   C turn yellow   D die   E grow

55 From the Earth: Greetings

Radio astronomy has greatly increased our understanding of the universe. Radio telescopes have one big advantage over conventional telescopes in that they can
5 operate in all weather conditions and can pick up signals coming from very distant stars. These signals are produced by colliding stars or nuclear reactions in outer space. The most powerful signals
10 that have been received have been emitted by what seem to be truly colossal stars which scientists have named 'quasars'. A better understanding of these pheno- mena may completely alter our concep-
15 tion of the nature of the universe. The radio telescope at Jodrell Bank in England was for many years the largest in the world. A new telescope, over twice the size, was recently built at Sugar Grove in West Virginia.

intelligent creatures would be able to understand

Astronomers no longer regard as fanciful the idea that they may one day
20 pick up signals which have been sent by intelligent beings on other worlds. This possibility gives rise to interesting speculations. Highly advanced civiliza- tions may have existed on other planets long before intelligent forms of life evolved on the earth. Conversely, intelligent beings which are just beginning to develop on remote worlds may be ready to pick up our signals in thousands of
25 years' time, or when life on earth has become extinct. Such speculations no longer belong to the realm of science fiction, for astronomers are now exploring the chances of communicating with living creatures (if they exist) on distant planets. This undertaking which has been named Project Ozma was begun in 1960, but it may take a great many years before results are obtained.
30 Aware of the fact that it would be impossible to wait thousands or millions of years to receive an answer from a distant planet, scientists engaged in Project Ozma are concentrating their attention on stars which are relatively close. One of the most likely stars is Tau Ceti which is eleven light years away. If signals from the earth were received by intelligent creatures on a planet circling this
35 star, we would have to wait twenty-two years for an answer. The Green Bank telescope in West Virginia has been specially designed to distinguish between random signals and signals which might be in code. Even if contact were eventually established, astronomers would not be able to rely on language to communicate with other beings. They would use mathematics as this is the
40 only truly universal language. Numbers have the same value anywhere. For this reason, intelligent creatures in any part of the universe would be able to understand a simple arithmetical sequence. They would be able to reply to our signals using similar methods. The next step would be to try to develop means for sending television pictures. A single picture would tell us more than thou-
45 sands of words. In an age when anything seems to be possible, it would be narrow-minded in the extreme to ridicule these attempts to find out if there is life in other parts of the universe.

Comprehension

Give short answers to these questions in your own words as far as possible. Use one complete sentence for each answer.

a In what way are radio telescopes superior to conventional telescopes?
b How are radio signals produced in outer space?
c What are the astronomers engaged in Project Ozma trying to do?

Vocabulary

Explain the meanings of the following words and phrases as they are used in the passage: conventional (l. 4); colliding (l. 8); alter our conception (ll. 14–15); speculations (l. 21); conversely (l. 23); has become extinct (l. 25); communicating (l. 27).

Précis

In not more than 80 words write an account of Project Ozma. Use your own words as far as possible. Do not include anything that is not in the last paragraph.

Composition

Write a composition in about 300 words on one of the following:
a Supposing the time came when we could send television pictures of life on earth to intelligent creatures on other planets. What sort of pictures do you think would be most interesting to them?
b The view from my window at night.

Letter-writing

You borrowed from a friend a travel guide which you are now returning. Write him a letter of about 100 words thanking him for having lent it to you and telling him how useful you found it.

Key Structures and Special Difficulties

Rewrite the following sentence without changing the meaning. Then refer to ll. 33–35.
Signals from the earth might be received by intelligent creatures on a planet circling this star and we would have to wait twenty-two years for any answer.
If signals from the earth . . .

Multiple Choice Questions

a Choose the one answer (A, B, C or D) which you think is correct in the following:
Which would be the simplest way of communicating with creatures in outer space?

A   Sending messages to them in English;
B   Sending simple arithmetical sequences;
C   Arranging a meeting-place somewhere in the universe;
D   Sending television pictures.

b Choose the two answers which you think are correct in each of the following:
1. *When the scientists . . . a signal in code, they will try to reply.*

A will receive   B have received   C receive   D may receive   E would receive

2. *Mathematics . . . the only truly universal language.*

A are   B were   C is   D have   E was

56

Read carefully the following passage and answer questions *i*, *ii* and *iii*.

The river which forms the eastern bound-
ary of our farm has always played an
important part in our lives. Without it
we could not make a living. There is only
5 enough spring water to supply the needs
of the house, so we have to pump from
the river for farm use. We tell the river
all our secrets. We know instinctively,
just as beekeepers with their bees, that
10 misfortune might overtake us if the
important events of our lives were not
related to it.

    We have special river birthday parties
in the summer. Sometimes we go up-
15 stream to a favourite backwater, sometimes we have our party at the boathouse,

just as beekeepers with their bees

which a predecessor of ours at the farm built in the meadow hard by the deepest
pool for swimming and diving. In a heat-wave we choose a midnight birthday
party and that is the most exciting of all. We welcome the seasons by the river-
20 side, crowning the youngest girl with flowers in the spring, holding a summer
festival on Midsummer Eve, giving thanks for the harvest in the autumn, and
throwing a holly wreath into the current in the winter.

    After a long period of rain the river may overflow its banks. This is a rare
occurrence as our climate seldom goes to extremes. We are lucky in that only
25 the lower fields, which make up a very small proportion of our farm, are affected
by flooding, but other farms are less favourably sited, and flooding can sometimes
spell disaster for their owners.

    One bad winter we watched the river creep up the lower meadows. All the
cattle had been moved into stalls and we stood to lose little. We were, however,
30 worried about our nearest neighbours, whose farm was low lying and who were
newcomers to the district. As the floods had put the telephone out of order, we
could not find out how they were managing. From an attic window we could
get a sweeping view of the river where their land joined ours, and at the most
critical juncture we took turns in watching that point. The first sign of disaster
35 was a dead sheep floating down. Next came a horse, swimming bravely, but we
were afraid that the strength of the current would prevent its landing anywhere
before it became exhausted. Suddenly a raft appeared, looking rather like
Noah's ark, carrying the whole family, a few hens, the dogs, a cat, and a bird in
a cage. We realized that they must have become unduly frightened by the
40 rising flood, for their house, which had sound foundations, would have stood
stoutly even if it had been almost submerged. The men of our family waded
down through our flooded meadows with boathooks, in the hope of being able
to grapple a corner of the raft and pull it out of the current towards our bank.
We still think it a miracle that they were able to do so.

i Give short answers to each of the following questions, in your own words as far as possible, using only material contained in the passage. Use *one* complete sentence for each answer.
a Why were the family so dependent on the river for their livelihood?
b For what occasions did they hold festivities by the river?
c In what was the position of their farm fortunate?

ii Choose *five* of the following words or phrases and give for each another word or phrase of similar meaning to that in which the word or phrase is used in the passage: instinctively (l. 8); overtake (l. 10); predecessor (l. 17); hard by (l. 17); in a heat-wave (l. 18); a rare occurrence (ll. 23–24); goes to extremes (l. 24); favourably (l. 26).

iii Give an account *in not more than 80 words* of the author's description of events during the bad flood, as narrated in the last paragraph. Do not include anything that is not in the passage, and use your own words as far as possible.

Composition
Write a composition on *one* of the following subjects; the length should be between 250 and 350 words.
a What the world would be like without newspapers, radio, films and television.
b 'It was a dark and gloomy street.' Continue the story of an adventure you had in this street.

Letter-writing
Write a letter of between 80 and 100 words in length on *one* of the following subjects. You should make the beginning and ending like those of an ordinary letter, but the address is not to be counted in the total number of words.
a You have accidentally broken a window of the house (or flat) next door. As your neighbour is not in when you call, write a letter of apology, offering to make good the damage.
b Write a letter inviting a friend to go with you to a theatre, opera or ballet performance.

(From the Lower Certificate in English Examination, June 1960)

Key Structures and Special Difficulties
Rewrite the following sentence without changing the meaning. Then refer to ll. 31–32.
There was no way of finding out how they were managing, for the floods had put the telephone out of order.
As the floods . . . we could . . .

Multiple Choice Questions
a Choose the one answer (A, B, C or D) which you think is correct in the following:
They took it in turns to watch at the window:

A   to see if the water level would get any higher;
B   in case their neighbours appeared;
C   to see if any dead animals would come floating down the river;
D   because their neighbours' farm was low-lying.

b Choose the two answers which are correct in the following:
Even if their house . . . it would have stood.

A   had been almost covered with water   B   was covered with water   C   had been flooded   D   is flooded   E   would be flooded

57

Read carefully the following passage and answer questions *i, ii* and *iii*.

I stopped to let the car cool off and to study the map. I had expected to be near my objective by now, but everything still seemed alien to me. I was only five when
5 my father had taken me abroad, and that was eighteen years ago. When my mother had died after a tragic accident, he did not quickly recover from the shock and loneliness. Everything around him was
10 full of her presence, continually re-opening the wound. So he decided to emigrate. In the new country he became absorbed in making a new life for the two of us, so that he gradually ceased to
15 grieve. He did not marry again and I was brought up without a woman's care; but

everything seemed alien

I lacked for nothing, for he was both father and mother to me. He always meant to go back one day, but not to stay. His roots and mine had become too firmly embedded in the new land. But he wanted to see the old folk again and to visit
20 my mother's grave. He became mortally ill a few months before we had planned to go and, when he knew that he was dying, he made me promise to go on my own.

I hired a car the day after landing and bought a comprehensive book of maps, which I found most helpful on the cross country journey, but which I did not
25 think I should need on the last stage. It was not that I actually remembered anything at all. But my father had described over and over again what we should see at every milestone, after leaving the nearest town, so that I was positive I should recognize it as familiar territory. Well, I had been wrong, for I was now lost.

30 I looked at the map and then at the milometer. I had come ten miles since leaving the town, and at this point, according to my father, I should be looking at farms and cottages in a valley, with the spire of the church of our village showing in the far distance. I could see no valley, no farms, no cottages and no church spire—only a lake. I decided that I must have taken a wrong turning
35 somewhere. So I drove back to the town and began to retrace the route, taking frequent glances at the map. I landed up at the same corner. The curious thing was that the lake was not marked on the map. I felt as if I had stumbled into a nightmare country, as you sometimes do in dreams. And, as in a nightmare, there was nobody in sight to help me. Fortunately for me, as I was wondering
40 what to do next, there appeared on the horizon a man on horseback, riding in my direction. I waited till he came near, then I asked him the way to our old village. He said that there was now no village. I thought he must have mis-understood me, so I repeated its name. This time he pointed to the lake. The

village no longer existed because it had been submerged, and all the valley too.
45 The lake was not a natural one, but a man made reservoir.

i Give short answers to each of the following questions in your own words as far as possible, using only material contained in the passage. Use *one* complete sentence for each answer.
a Why did the author's father emigrate?
b Why had the author come back to the land of his birth?
c What made the author think that he would not need a map for the last part of his journey?

ii Choose *five* of the following words and phrases and give for each another word or phrase of similar meaning to that in which the word or phrase is used in the passage: objective (l. 3); seemed alien (l. 4); lacked for nothing (l. 17); embedded (l. 19); mortally (l. 20); comprehensive (l. 23); positive (l. 27); familiar territory (l. 28).

iii Give an account *in not more than 80 words* of the author's search for the village, as narrated in the last paragraph. Use your own words as far as possible. Do not include anything that is not in the paragraph.

Composition
Write a composition on *one* of the following subjects; the length should be between 250 and 350 words.
a The house you wish to own.
b A day spent by the sea or by a lake or river.

Letter-writing
Write a letter between 80 and 100 words in length on *one* of the following subjects. You should make the beginning and ending like those of an ordinary letter. Write the postal address in full at the head of your letter, but do not count this address in the total number of words.
a You are ill and cannot go to work for a few days. Write explaining your absence and making arrangements for your work while you are absent.
b You have received a gift from an old friend abroad. Write a letter of thanks, say how you will make use of the gift and briefly give news of yourself.

(From the Lower Certificate in English Examination, June 1961)

Key Structures and Special Difficulties
Rewrite the following sentence without changing the meaning. Then refer to ll. 33–34.
It wasn't possible for me to see any valley, any farms, any cottages and any church spire— only a lake.
I could see . . .

Multiple Choice Questions
Choose the one answer which you think is correct in the following:
The stranger who appeared on horseback told the author that:
  A   there had never been a village;
  B   he had made a mistake about the village;
  C   the lake was a natural reservoir;
  D   the village had been covered by water.

58

Read carefully the following passage and answer questions *i*, *ii* and *iii*.

what she described as a little spot of bother

The old lady was glad to be back at the block of flats where she lived. Her shopping had tired her and her basket had grown heavier with every step of the way
5 home. In the lift her thoughts were on lunch and a good rest; but when she got out at her own floor, both were forgotten in her sudden discovery that her front door was open. She was thinking that she
10 must reprimand her daily maid the next morning for such a monstrous piece of negligence, when she remembered that she had gone shopping after the maid had left and she knew that she had turned
15 both keys in their locks. She walked slowly into the hall and at once noticed that all the room doors were open, yet following her regular practice she had shut them before going out. Looking into the drawing room, she saw a scene of confusion over by her writing desk. It was as clear as daylight then that burglars
20 had forced an entry during her absence. Her first impulse was to go round all the rooms looking for the thieves, but then she decided that at her age it might be more prudent to have someone with her, so she went to fetch the porter from his basement. By this time her legs were beginning to tremble, so she sat down and accepted a cup of very strong tea, while he telephoned the police. Then,
25 her composure regained, she was ready to set off with the porter's assistance to search for any intruders who might still be lurking in her flat.

They went through the rooms, being careful to touch nothing, as they did not want to hinder the police in their search for fingerprints. The chaos was inconceivable. She had lived in the flat for thirty years and was a veritable
30 magpie at hoarding; and it seemed as though everything she possessed had been tossed out and turned over and over. At least sorting out the things she should have discarded years ago was now being made easier for her. Then a police inspector arrived with a constable and she told them of her discovery of the ransacked flat. The inspector began to look for fingerprints, while the
35 constable checked that the front door locks had not been forced, thereby proving that the burglars had either used skeleton keys or entered over the balcony. There was no trace of fingerprints, but the inspector found a dirty red bundle that contained jewellery which the old lady said was not hers. So their entry into this flat was apparently not the burglars' first job that day and they
40 must have been disturbed. The inspector then asked the old lady to try to check what was missing by the next day and advised her not to stay alone in the flat for a few nights. The old lady thought he was a fussy creature, but since the porter agreed with him, she rang up her daughter and asked for her help in what she described as a little spot of bother.

i Give short answers to each of the following questions, in your own words as far as possible, using only material contained in the passage. Use *one* complete sentence for each answer.
a Why was the old lady surprised to find her front door open?
b What made her realize that burglars had entered the flat?
c Why did she go down to the basement?

ii Choose *five* of the following words and phrases and give for each another word or phrase of similar meaning to that in which the word or phrase is used in the passage: reprimand (l. 10); piece of negligence (ll. 11–12); regular practice (l. 17); as clear as daylight (l. 19); prudent (l. 22); her composure regained (l. 25); intruders (l. 26); lurking (l. 26).

(iii) Give an account *in not more than 80 words* of what took place in the flat after the old lady had returned to it with the porter. Use your own words as far as possible. Do not include anything that is not in the last paragraph.

Composition
Write a composition on *one* of the following subjects; the length should be between 250 and 350 words.
a Public festivals in your own country.
b Your adventures when you first visited a foreign country.

Letter-writing
Write a letter of between 80 and 100 words in length on *one* of the following subjects. You should make the beginning and ending like those of an ordinary letter, but the address is not to be counted in the total number of words.
a You are ill and cannot meet a friend (who has no telephone) as arranged. Write explaining why you cannot meet, and invite him or her to visit you.
b An English friend has written asking you to help in finding, for a seventeen-year-old English student, a school or place for training or study in your country. Answer the letter giving any helpful information.

(From the Lower Certificate in English Examination, June 1962)

Key Structures and Special Difficulties
Rewrite the following sentence without changing the meaning. Then refer to ll. 40–42.
  '*Try to check what's missing by tomorrow and don't stay alone in the flat for a few nights,*' *the inspector said.*
  The inspector asked the old lady . . . and advised her . . .

Multiple Choice Questions
Choose the two answers which you think are correct in each of the following:
  1. *The old lady had lots of things she . . . years ago.*

  A had to throw away   B must have thrown away   C ought to have thrown away
  D should have thrown away   E might have thrown away

  2. *As soon as the inspector and the constable arrived they . . .*

  A asked the lady questions   B checked the locks   C gave the lady some advice
  D looked for fingerprints   E proved that the burglars had used skeleton keys

59

Read carefully the following passage and answer questions *i*, *ii* and *iii*.

People tend to amass possessions, sometimes without being aware of doing so.
Indeed they can have a delightful surprise
when they find something useful which
5 they did not know they owned. Those
who never have to change house become
indiscriminate collectors of what can only
be described as clutter. They leave un-
wanted objects in drawers, cupboards and
10 attics for years, in the belief that they
may one day need just those very things.
As they grow old, people also accumulate
belongings for two other reasons, lack of
physical and mental energy, both of
15 which are essential in turning out and
throwing away, and sentiment. Things

associations with the past

owned for a long time are full of associations with the past, perhaps with relatives
who are dead, and so they gradually acquire a value beyond their true worth.

Some things are collected deliberately in the home in an attempt to avoid
20 waste. Among these I would list string and brown paper, kept by thrifty people
when a parcel has been opened, to save buying these two requisites. Collecting
small items can easily become a mania. I know someone who always cuts out
from newspapers sketches of model clothes that she would like to buy, if she had
the money. As she is not rich, the chances that she will ever be able to afford
25 such purchases are remote; but she is never sufficiently strongminded to be
able to stop the practice. It is a harmless habit, but it litters up her desk to such
an extent that every time she opens it, loose bits of paper fall out in every
direction.

Collecting as a serious hobby is quite different and has many advantages. It
30 provides relaxation for leisure hours, as just looking at one's treasures is always
a joy. One does not have to go outside for amusement, since the collection is
housed at home. Whatever it consists of, stamps, records, first editions of books,
china, glass, antique furniture, pictures, model cars, stuffed birds, toy animals,
there is always something to do in connection with it, from finding the right
35 place for the latest addition to verifying facts in reference books. This hobby
educates one not only in the chosen subject, but also in general matters which
have some bearing on it. There are also other benefits. One wants to meet
like-minded collectors, to get advice, to compare notes, to exchange articles, to
show off the latest find. So one's circle of friends grows. Soon the hobby leads
40 to travel, perhaps to a meeting in another town, possibly a trip abroad in search
of a rare specimen, for collectors are not confined to any one country. Over the
years one may well become an authority on one's hobby and will very probably
be asked to give informal talks to little gatherings and then, if successful, to
larger audiences. In this way self-confidence grows, first from mastering a

subject, then from being able to talk about it. Collecting, by occupying spare time so constructively, makes a person contented, with no time for boredom.

i Give short answers to each of the following questions, in your own words as far as possible, using only material contained in the passage. Use *one* complete sentence for each answer.
a Why do some people tend to hoard things which they never use?
b What special reasons cause old people to keep possessions which they no longer need?
c Why was it not very sensible of the author's friend to collect sketches of model clothes?

ii Choose *five* of the following words and phrases and give for each another word or phrase of similar meaning to that in which the word or phrase is used in the passage: amass (l. 1); being aware (l. 2); change house (l. 6); attics (l. 10); gradually acquire (l. 18); thrifty (l. 20); in every direction (ll. 27–28).

iii Give an account *in not more than 80 words* of the advantages which the author attributes to having collecting as a hobby. Use your own words as far as possible. Do not include anything that is not in the last paragraph.

Composition
Write a composition on *one* of the following subjects; the length should be between 250 and 350 words.
a If you could choose, in which country would you like to live and why?
b Write a short story beginning 'There was a knock on the window . . .'

Letter-writing
Write a letter of between 80 and 100 words in length on *one* of the following subjects. You should make the beginning and ending like those of an ordinary letter, but the address is not to be counted in the total number of words.
a A friend is coming to visit you. Write a short letter giving him (or her) directions for finding your house.
b Write a letter to a friend explaining that, through illness, you will be unable to go to stay with him (or her) as previously arranged. Say how you are progressing and suggest alternative arrangements.

(From the Lower Certificate in English Examination, June 1964)

Key Structures and Special Difficulties
Rewrite the following sentence without changing the meaning. Then refer to ll. 41–42.
Over the years it is quite likely that one will become an authority on one's hobby.
Over the years one . . .

Multiple Choice Questions
Choose the one answer which is correct in the following:
Why is it likely that you will travel if you are a collector?

A   Because you may have to go to a meeting or in search of a rare specimen;
B   Because you may want to consult a reference book;
C   Because you want to occupy your time constructively;
D   Because this is one of the benefits of collecting things.

Read carefully the following passage and answer questions *i*, *ii* and *iii*.

Punctuality is a necessary habit in all public affairs of a civilized society. Without it, nothing could ever be brought to a conclusion; everything would be in a
5 state of chaos. Only in a sparsely-populated rural community is it possible to disregard it. In ordinary living there can be some tolerance of unpunctuality. The intellectual, who is working on some
10 abstruse problem, has everything co-ordinated and organized for the matter in hand. He is therefore forgiven, if late for a dinner party. But people are often reproached for unpunctuality when their
15 only fault is cutting things fine. It is hard for energetic, quick-minded people to

half an hour too soon

waste time, so they are often tempted to finish a job before setting out to keep an appointment. If no accidents occur on the way, like punctured tyres, diversions of traffic, sudden descent of fog, they will be on time. They are often more
20 industrious, useful citizens than those who are never late. The over-punctual can be as much a trial to others as the unpunctual. The guest who arrives half an hour too soon is the greatest nuisance. Some friends of my family had this irritating habit. The only thing to do was ask them to come half an hour later than the other guests. Then they arrived just when we wanted them.
25 If you are catching a train, it is always better to be comfortably early than even a fraction of a minute too late. Although being early may mean wasting a little time, this will be less than if you miss the train and have to wait an hour or more for the next one; and you avoid the frustration of arriving at the very moment when the train is drawing out of the station and being unable to get on
30 it. An even harder situation is to be on the platform in good time for a train and still to see it go off without you. Such an experience befell a certain young girl the first time she was travelling alone.
She entered the station twenty minutes before the train was due, since her parents had impressed upon her that it would be unforgivable to miss it and
35 cause the friends with whom she was going to stay to make two journeys to meet her. She gave her luggage to a porter and showed him her ticket. To her horror he said that she was two hours too soon. She felt in her handbag for the piece of paper on which her father had written down all the details of the journey and gave it to the porter. He agreed that a train did come into the station
40 at the time on the paper and that it did stop, but only to take on water, not passengers. The girl asked to see a timetable, feeling sure that her father could not have made such a mistake. The porter went to fetch one and arrived back with the stationmaster, who produced it with a flourish and pointed out a microscopic 'o' beside the time of the arrival of the train at his station; this

little 'o' indicated that the train only stopped for water. Just as that moment the train came into the station. The girl, tears streaming down her face, begged to be allowed to slip into the guard's van. But the stationmaster was adamant: rules could not be broken. And she had to watch that train disappear towards her destination while she was left behind.

i Give short answers to each of the following questions, in your own words as far as possible, using only material contained in the passage. Use *one* complete sentence for each answer.
a What are the dangers of leaving the bare minimum of time for appointments?
b Why did the author's family ask some guests to come half an hour later than others invited for the same day?
c Why, according to the author, is it better to choose to wait on the platform before the train arrives than to be forced to wait after it has gone?

ii Choose *five* of the following words and phrases and give for each another word or phrase of similar meaning to that in which the word or phrase is used in the passage: a state of chaos (ll. 4–5); sparsely-populated (ll. 5–6); disregard (l. 7): reproached (l. 14); setting out (l. 17); diversions (ll. 18–19); industrious (l. 20); destination (l. 49).

iii Give an account *in not more than 80 words* of the girl's experience on the railway station, when she was not allowed to get on the train. Do not include anything that is not in the last paragraph. Use your own words as far as possible.

Composition
Write a composition on *one* of the following subjects; the length should be between 250 and 350 words.
a Write a short story beginning 'A piece of paper was blowing in the wind . . .'
b What science has done to make our lives easier and more comfortable.

Letter-writing
Write a letter of between 80 and 100 words in length on *one* of the following subjects. You should make the beginning and ending like those of an ordinary letter, but the address is not to be counted in the total number of words.
a Write a letter informing your employer (or the Principal of your School) that you have to be absent for a few days and explaining why this is necessary.
b A friend with several young children has fallen ill. Write offering help or suggesting a way in which help can be obtained.

(From the Lower Certificate in English Examination, December 1964)

Key Structures and Special Difficulties
Rewrite the following sentence without changing the meaning. Then refer to l. 41.
   'May I see the timetable, please?' the girl asked.
   The girl asked to . . .

Multiple Choice Questions
Choose the two answers which are correct in the following:
   The girl felt sure that her father couldn't . . .

   A have been right   B have seen the timetable   C have been wrong   D have noticed the 'o' beside the time of arrival   E have been mistaken